the
LEADER'S
wife

ENDORSEMENTS

I am the wife of a leader and understand the feelings, fears, and failings of others like me. My dear friend Debby Thompson has written a GPS just for us! *The Leader's Wife* is your "go to book"—it will empower you with definition and direction in becoming the person and partner you long to be! Read this book! It is life changing!

– LINDA DILLOW

Author of *Calm My Anxious Heart, What's it Like to be Married to Me?*, and coauthor of *Intimate Issues*

At last, here is help for a very strategic and influential segment of the Christian community! Debby Thompson, in her ground-breaking book, *The Leader's Wife*, offers honest, thoughtful and practical insights to help empower wives of leaders who want to face their unique challenges with intentionality and confidence.

We have known Debby for almost 40 years and have watched as she bravely trusted God in some very difficult situations and observed how she has supported and partnered with her leader husband, Larry, literally all over the world. This book will be a must read for any woman who is married to a leader.

– DAVID & CLAUDIA ARP

Authors of the *10 Great Dates* series including *10 Great Dates: Connecting Faith, Love & Marriage*

Few women are as qualified as Debby Thompson to write *The Leader's Wife*. For one thing she is married to a leader, a proven, high-energy risk taking leader who accepts no limits for his vision and gives everything he has every day to his Lord. For another, she has lived everything she writes in this book. She is not a theorist, an armchair researcher. Her research comes out of the crucible of living for the Gospel under Communist rule, out of the crushing demands of raising three children while living in four cultures and struggling with foreign languages and radically different expectations. She has experienced it all with her husband: the joy, the stress and pressure of supernatural demands, the exaltation of supernatural answers, the loneliness of being home alone while he travels, the excitement of significant achievements, the criticism, the resentment when tough decisions have to be made and undesired directions must be taken. Debby knows what she is talking about.

And she says it well, really well, through story, teaching, illustration, and vulnerability all brought together by a heart for her readers. One of the things that makes Debby such an effective writer is her desire for those she serves. She writes this book out of concern for her readers because she has a burden for those who are confused and uncertain and don't know what to do with their leader husbands. Her encouraging empathy for them comes through in her identification with them and her exhortation for their growth and joy in marriage. She sees her role as a privilege, not as a painful burden that she must bear.

Leaders and their wives will benefit greatly from this well crafted and challenging word that comes from one of them, not as a wagging finger or a bleeding heart, but with the compassionate insight of a realist who knows all their struggles, who struggles with them, and who loves them as few can.

– Dr. Bill & Lynna Lawrence
Leader Formation, International

I've known Debby Thompson for quite a few decades. I have enjoyed meals, coffee, dinner on the Danube, and many long conversations with this delightful woman of God. I have watched her lead the women God has entrusted to her, listen to their hearts, share her heart. I have heard her speak and encourage and pray. I have admired how she has partnered with Larry to lead thousands of men and women, often in difficult situations, in different languages and countries, guiding them to the place of help and hope—to Jesus.

This book is not theory. It is lived out experience. It is love in action. Debby Thompson is the right woman to write it. You will be glad when you read it.

– Judy Douglass
Encourager, Writer, Speaker
Director of Women's Resources
Partner with Steve in leading Cru

Debby Thompson has written a book that will be water to the soul of women longing for sympathy, compassion, and direction in their lives as they partner with their husbands in leadership positions in ministry. The book is filled with heart-felt stories, sound encouragement, and inspiration. She touches on the deep issues that women carry and stands beside them as an experienced mentor. A must read for all women in ministry who want to flourish.

– SALLY CLARKSON

Author of numerous books including *Own Your Life*, a conference speaker, and a popular blogger at sallyclarkson.com

Debby Thompson has served extremely well as the wife of a Christian leader. She has made a strong contribution to his success. She not only provides some complementary strengths to him but also blends them in with humility, grace, and joy. On top of that, in her own right, she makes excellent contributions to our ministry and to the lives of the people around her. I trust you will be blessed by her transparent style and excellent, practical ideas.

– STEVE DOUGLASS

President, Campus Crusade for Christ, International

The Leader's Wife—What an insightful book for millennials! We serve in a busy environment of social media, travel, family, and work. Seeking a unified marriage grounded in God's Word, we love the challenge that Debby Thompson provides with humor, candor, and a clarifying focus on Christ in all aspects of a marriage. Speaking from her heart and life, her challenge to your heart, will encourage you to connect truth to your marriage and provide practical steps to strengthen the vital relationship that God entrusts to you with your spouse.

– DAVID THOMPSON & BETH THOMPSON

Samaritan's Purse

Senior Director of Operation Christmas Child International

Medical Program Specialist, Nurse

My excitement grew as I read *The Leader's Wife: Living With Eternal Intentionality.* I not only soaked in godly wisdom and truth, but my heart soared with hope as I pondered the far reaching, kingdom impact of Debby Thompson's work. She gets it! We as women have profound influence and to realize the transformational potential for us to become all that God intended is simply powerful.

– ESTHER FETHERLIN

Wife and partner in ministry with Bob Fetherlin,
President of One Mission Society

Years ago, someone once told me, "It is lonely at the top." At the time it was a fleeting comment, but now as the wife of a senior military leader, it is accurate. Quite often the wife is left on her own with very little guidance or direction. Debby Thompson touches on issues, thoughts, and feelings that I regularly wrestle with as the wife of a leader in her book *The Leader's Wife.* God has been and continues to be my stronghold, but *The Leader's Wife* provides me with inspiration and encouragement from a godly woman who knows first-hand the challenges we face. Many wives of leaders suffer in silence for a variety of reasons, but Debby's book exposes, not only the suffering, but also the loneliness that so many of us endure. This book establishes a God-centered road map equipping me to walk side by side with my world-changing husband.

I first met Debby twenty years ago in Budapest at a small International Church. She invited me, along with other American women living in the city, to a Bible study she was leading. Her Bible studies were life changing and critical for many of us living in a foreign country. She is filled with God's love, a passion for women's hearts, and is an exceptional communicator. *The Leader's Wife* provides reassurance of knowing that I am not alone in my doubts and feelings as the wife of a leader. Thank you, Debby, for this intimately personal resource that is desperately needed in today's world!

– MARGARET BRIGGS

Spouse of JL Briggs, Maj Gen, USAF (Ret)

Debby Thompson has lived the reality of these principles for many decades as the wife of a world-changing leader. She has done so with strength, consistency, and winsome character. I highly recommend that women comb through the pages of this book and glean from Debby's valuable words and experience. Truly, this is a unique opportunity to learn and be changed by an exemplary life.

– MARY HENDERSON

Licensed Marriage and Family Therapist

Author of *Break Free* and *Retrain Your Brain for Joy*

This book answers the heart cry of many wives of gospel-minded, ministry leaders . . . "while he is changing the world, where do I fit in?" Debby responds with tenderness, understanding, and compassion as she urges each wife to not just buck up under the load, but to recognize God's holy call on her life and to join in the work that He has given her to do. Debby dares to go where few have gone before honestly and openly encouraging wives to love their husbands well. I have several women in mind already that I will give this book to when it is in print, and I look forward to seeing its impact for the kingdom of God.

– DR. JAYNE CUIDON

Co-author of *Building Your Child through Love and Trust* and co-director of the Barnabas Zentrum, a counseling center for those in full-time ministry

We have such great respect for Debby Thompson. She draws on forty years of fruitful ministry experience with her husband Larry to write a much-needed book. We have known Debby to be a very effective leader herself, reflecting a heart for God, a commitment to prayer and always full of faith. Her effective partnership with Larry has resulted in immeasurable Kingdom impact. This book will be a gift to many in years to come.

– MARK & MARIANNE HOUSEHOLDER

President, Athletes in Action

As a staff member with Campus Crusade for Christ for 40 years, Debby Thompson is uniquely qualified to write *The Leader's Wife*. Through each chapter Debby expertly ministers guidance, encouragement, and hope to wives of spiritual leaders through a combination of her own personal experiences, Scripture, and cameos of wives of famous leaders. Her passion and skill to mentor women married to world-changers is evident on every page. She tackles tough issues with a deftness that comes from her 30 years as a missionary spouse behind the Iron Curtain. Her down-to-earth advice rings with the warmth and candor of a confidante enjoying a cup of tea with a friend while discussing the challenges common to wives of Christian leaders. Debby empowers and equips her readers with grace, love, and practical suggestions to deal with the complexities inherent in their unique calling as helpmates to pastors, missionaries, seminary students, church planters, or para-church leaders.

– JANE GLENCHUR

Author of *Seven Secrets to Power Praying*

Debby Thompson writes a deeply personal and profoundly relevant manual for wives of all kinds of Christian leaders. An alternate title could be, "More Than His Wife: how to serve alongside your husband while remaining the woman God designed you to be." Drawing on years of experience, she offers insights that are both helpful and hopeful for women who are "often in the line of fire when the bullets start flying." Her work will be appreciated by families and ministries— and, most importantly, women—around the world.

– SUSIE THOMAS

Grade 5 teacher, co-founder of B2theworld,

Wife of Ben Thomas, Director of Kigali International Community School, Kigali, Rwanda

Debby Thompson, my dear friend of 35 years, has a genuine heart to help you. She is not only the devoted wife of a leader, but a significant leader in her own right. In a warm, loving transparent way, Debby will lead you along sensitive, vulnerable pathways helping you discern possible pitfalls as the wife of a leader. And she will lead you with sensitivity and understanding. I highly recommend her book, *The Leader's Wife*.

– NEY BAILEY

Author, Speaker

Cru, Campus Crusade for Christ, International

As a follower of Jesus and a leader in ministry for over 30 years, I know the best way I can live and lead is in close partnership with my wife. Debby Thompson draws from her life and experiences coming alongside thousands of women (including Dana, my wife) in providing an encouraging, heartfelt and biblical road map for wives of leaders (and their husbands too!) to anchor their identity in Christ and expand their influence for the Kingdom. I heartily encourage you to journey with Debby through the pages of *The Leader's Wife: Living With Eternal Intentionality*. You'll be challenged to love Jesus more deeply and live more boldly in following the Leader of leaders, Jesus.

– DR. RICK FRANKLIN

Vice President, Arrow Leadership Ministries

You can be used by God uniquely and partner with your husband. Debby's experience and wisdom are infused into this gem of a book and will lead you through a journey of growth and discovery producing greater intimacy with God and fulfilling partnership with your husband.

– DANA FRANKLIN

Program Associate, Arrow Leadership Ministries

I've waited for this book for 10 years, since Debby spoke on this topic at our women's conference in Ukraine.

– KARA COE

Missional leader's wife, St. Petersburg, Russia

With the very first page, I found my spirit resonating with what was written. Why? Because my own dear wife has experienced so many of the challenges Debby addresses. Debby provides counsel and encouragement through the Scriptures and the examples of famous, godly wives, while always pointing us back to our relationship with Jesus. This book meets a need that I've yet to see addressed in print!

– GREG ST. CYR

Pastor of Bay Area Community Church

Annapolis, Maryland

the LEADER'S *wife*

Living with
ETERNAL INTENTIONALITY™

Debby Thompson

AMBASSADOR INTERNATIONAL
GREENVILLE, SOUTH CAROLINA & BELFAST, NORTHERN IRELAND

www.ambassador-international.com

The Leader's Wife
Living with Eternal Intentionality

Hardcover ISBN: 978-1-64960-291-6
Paperback ISBN: 978-1-62020-616-4
eISBN: 978-1-62020-695-9

Cover Design and Interior Layout by Hannah Nichols
Author Photo by Joel Phaler

AMBASSADOR INTERNATIONAL
Emerald House Group, Inc.
411 University Ridge, Suite B14
Greenville, SC 29601
United States
www.ambassador-international.com

AMBASSADOR BOOKS
The Mount
2 Woodstock Link
Belfast, BT6 8DD
Northern Ireland, United Kingdom
www.ambassadormedia.co.uk

The colophon is a trademark of Ambassador, a Christian publishing company.

To Jesus

Apart from You, I can do nothing.

John 15:5

You gave me a life worth living and a story worth telling.

To Larry

My gift to you for our 45th wedding anniversary

I am forever grateful for your proposal,

"Will you go with me in helping to reach the world for Christ?"

CONTENTS

FOREWORD 17

GETTING ACQUAINTED 19

Person

Chapter 1
RENDEZVOUS WITH REALITY 25

Chapter 2
NOT *JUST* MRS. LARRY THOMPSON 29

Chapter 3
LONGING FOR A BURNING HEART 43

Chapter 4
GROWTH IS FOR GROWN-UPS 59

Partner

Chapter 5
A ROCK STAR REINTRODUCED 75

Chapter 6
PLAYING DOUBLES 89

Portrait

Chapter 7
PONDERING TWO PORTRAITS
101

Chapter 8
PAINTING TWO PORTRAITS
111

Chapter 9
NO NEED FOR BATHSHEBA
123

Promises

Chapter 10
PROMISES, POWERFUL PROMISES FOR YOU, THE LEADER'S WIFE
139

APPENDIX
155

NOTES
171

ABOUT THE AUTHOR
173

ACKNOWLEDGMENTS
175

FOREWORD

MY DEAR FRIEND, DEBBY IS now a grandmother of six, but I first knew her as a mother of little ones living behind the Iron Curtain in Communist Poland. Our family living in Vienna, Austria, had the joy of being the Thompson's "home away from home" when they traveled out of Poland. As I think back to those years, my mind is filled with so many memories of . . .

Baby David being guarded in his playpen by our fluffy white dog, Tasha. She was especially vigilant when Daddy Larry playfully threw David high in the air!

Debby's very wonderful, and *very* southern Mama calling during martial law in Poland and asking with agonizing gasps, "Linda, Linda, where are my babies? Can you tell them to get my babies out of that country!"

Debby and me shop, shop, shopping until their van was filled to the brim with toilet paper, rice, powdered milk, coffee, oatmeal . . . really EVERYTHING for a family of five as the stores in Poland had little food.

Now my friend, Debby has written this book especially for *YOU*, the wife of a leader. With personal honesty, humor, and vulnerability, Debby takes you on a journey to clarify and equip you as a person and as a partner. She lived out being a leader's wife in four different countries, with four different languages. I was pulled in with her words, *I write not as an expert, but as an experienced mentor.* And I will add that her words about remaining time-challenged made me laugh!

"The Big Clock App will perpetually be needed on my iPhone. I will always be glad when you are not early to my front door. I promise promptness for the Rapture or for my own funeral, depending on which comes first."

I've been the wife of a leader for 53 years. The words in this book gave me renewed motivation to walk out truths I know, said in fresh "Debby speak" like these four sentences I'm going to put on a little plaque in my office:

To look down is to be discouraged.

To look around is to be disappointed.

To look within is to be disillusioned.

To look up is to see Him!

I needed to read Debby's book and I've made a list of fifteen women I am buying it for; I know the list will grow.

I highly recommend *The Leader's Wife: Living with Eternal Intentionality* to you!

—LINDA DILLOW

Author, *Calm My Anxious Heart, Creative Counterpart,* and *What's it Like to be Married to Me?*

GETTING ACQUAINTED

HI, I'M DEBBY. THANK YOU for joining me here on a journey of the heart. With a passion for Jesus and a precision of purpose, I write—not as an expert, but as a mentor, an experienced mentor.

As I meet women around the world who, like you, live with world-changers, I ask the question: *What is one of the greatest challenges you face as a leader's wife?*

Some have said:

> I feel so alone. Is there a place for me? Satan feeds me lies. I am tired of being alone.

> Dealing with gossip, criticism, and unrealistic expectations of my husband, our children, or myself.

> Being transparent, especially when I (or we) are hurting and dealing with challenges that should not be shared with everyone.

> It has been a challenge to find that childcare falls to me, or that I must bring up the topic of alternatives so I can engage on a functional ministry level.

> Responding to people who come to me to get to my husband. They will not approach him, but will talk to me to get a "message" to him.

> It is a battle to live in contentment and thanksgiving without worry and fear.

Financial challenges . . . often the pay is not adequate for the needs of raising a family.

Truthfully, I've never even had anyone ask me this question.

Criticism: it's horrid, especially when it comes from friends you've confided in, people you do life with.

One of the most difficult experiences that I have encountered was being part of a very close church family where I was aware that there was opposition to my husband and his ministry. This opposition was very obvious. To be free to love the Lord and serve Him in this situation was very difficult for me.

Hard. It is just so hard.

I feel a sense of needing or wanting to protect my husband, especially when (not if) he is under attack. But I can't fight his battles for him.

The job my husband does never seems to have a beginning or an end. It's a constant companion. It's a dull hum that rises and falls; at times to a fevered pitch and at times merely a quiet murmur in the background. But always there. It's been attention hungry and difficult to tame over the years. Tiredness and weariness are some of its fruits. This of course is the darker side of ministry, which includes a bright side of fulfillment and joy in following the call of God and living out of the gifts that God has given.

There are numerous blessings in being the leader's wife. But that also brings increased responsibility and accountability because people are watching. I have to be extra careful about my words and actions as well as what I wear, watch, read, and eat.

Sitting by his side even when I am not in agreement with him and his opinion or position.

To hear criticism of my husband and to accept it with grace— not allow it to color my thinking about that person.

Leadership can be and often is lonely for both spouses.

To be informed and abreast of his mental inner workings, dreams for the future, and direction we are headed.

Leaders, by virtue of their position, are often criticized. It's important to not only help one's spouse discern the truth, but also empathize, all the while not taking into oneself that criticism . . . remembering to hold it for yourself and your spouse open-handedly before the Lord, asking for His Voice.

Let me pause here and ask for your feedback. As you read through these comments, do you hear your own voice? Do you identify with one particular answer or can you relate to several?

Your response matters to me. In fact, this volume is designed uniquely for you, one married to a world-changer. As a woman who leads a life of impact and influence—extraordinary influence—I am concerned that, perhaps, you find yourself going through life without clarity and equipping.

Designed as both a tool and a weapon, *The Leader's Wife* serves as a tool to help you become all that God created you to become, and a weapon to arm you against the enemy of your soul. Through Biblical teaching and cutting-edge life lessons, the content sets out to provide you with definition and direction, so that as a person and as a partner you, too, can lead with confidence, intentionality, and expertise.

Let me reiterate: here I offer, not a job description, but a *GPS*, not a to do, but a to become, not a how to—have to, must do, ought to—but a directional compass. Your name is inscribed on every page.

Now, I embark on a venture to pass on what I have learned. Between these covers, you and I address some of the most difficult questions facing the leader's wife. With vulnerability, I candidly share my mistakes.

Where are we headed? Four words serve as navigational pathfinders: person, partner, portrait, and promises. We begin by discussing your incomprehensible beauty and worth as a *person*. (After all, God created you as a *person* long before you became a wife.) Then, the challenges you face as a *partner* in being married to a leader take focus. Later, we gaze at God's glorious *portrait* for oneness. Finally, together you and I embrace and celebrate His arsenal of *promises*, which empower us to pursue excellence, camaraderie, and companionship in marriage.

Abraham Lincoln is credited with saying, "Behind every good man is a good woman." Respectfully, I disagree with this statement by the sixteenth President of the United States, and I disagree with its philosophy. Personally, I believe God designed me to walk beside my husband, not behind him, to share life, embrace life, and face life *together*. Does this resonate within you as well?

I yearn to encourage you to maximize your own individual life so that you live in the *sweet spot* for which you were created. In that *sweet spot* I envision that you will experience:

Intimacy with Jesus

Authenticity with others

A passion for your calling

A purpose for your influence

As you and I together walk and talk with Him, and share life one page after another, I desperately hope our hearts, too, burn within us (Luke 24:32). At journey's end, with conviction, may we convincingly declare: *Jesus plus nothing is more than enough; Jesus plus nothing is everything.*

Person

Chapter 1

RENDEZVOUS WITH REALITY

I NEVER KNEW WHAT I was supposed to do. (Silence) *I never knew my contribution.* (More silence.)

Her quivering voice and teary eyes spoke of a deep, hidden pain. Her husband's shoulders slumped. He took a breath and exhaled slowly, before looking to see if anyone could throw an emotional lifeline to his wife. Awkwardly, those of us seated nearby lowered our gaze. No one knew how to respond, and her two painful, vulnerable statements simply hung in the air.

Forthwith, the international conference for couples in leadership derailed. The carefully crafted agenda seemed unable to address the pain and confusion for the wife of one of its leaders.

As I listened, her two sentences gripped my heart, and I made a commitment: *By God's grace, I commit to share what I know, to impart lessons I've learned.* I knew hers was not an isolated voice, rather a consistent chorus of women from around the world who live life with world-changers. That day, my existing passion for this subject intersected with my friend's desperate plea for help. The convergence became the volume you hold.

To restate, this book is not a job description, but a *GPS*; not a to do, but a to become; not a how to, must do, but a directional compass. Let me explain.

Personally, I am married to a leader with a capital L. Larry's marriage proposal asked: *Will you go with me in helping to reach the world for Christ?* My answer, *yes,* catapulted me into an extraordinary journey (which continues to this day) of life lived alongside a world-changer.

Return with me to Thanksgiving night, November 25, 1972—I still feel the gentle rock of the swing where we sat outdoors at my parents' Southern home.

I shivered, though not because of the autumn air. Throughout this day I had sensed Larry on the verge of asking me to marry him, but his words never materialized. Finally, the moment emerged. I listened breathlessly, as he spoke: "God said that it is not good for man to be alone. Will you go with me in helping to reach the world for Christ?"

Wanting to savor every aspect of the momentous occasion, I exclaimed, "That is wonderful! Will you ask me again?" Later, I drifted to sleep in my yellow childhood bedroom, and I recalled a previous conversation with my college roommate: "Whoever marries Larry Thompson is the luckiest girl on earth." Now, I was to be that girl.

The proposal in the swing culminated an eighteen-month dating relationship. We met as students at Mississippi State University, where we both basked in the realization of our childhood dreams—he the football player and I the cheerleader. Now God placed another dream on our hearts—the dream of helping to fulfill the Great Commission from Matthew 28:18-20.

Individually and separately, we responded to the clarion call, *Come help change the world.* Nothing seemed worthier of our lives; joyfully, God's plan confirmed our living it out together.

Our wedding portrayed an unequivocal commitment to the Lord, to each other, and to God's calling on our lives. The ceremony occurred in a small country church, where the soft glow of candles and the scent of homegrown gardenias created a heaven-like atmosphere. The words in the final congregational hymn before family and friends, "We Have Decided to Follow Jesus . . . no turning back, no turning back," served to declare our genuine devotion. Yet no one, not even the bride and groom, could fathom its far-reaching effect.

A dramatic vision two weeks earlier altered forever the course of our lives.

The Vision

The supernatural vision for Eastern Europe and Russia unexpectedly gripped Larry while working in his summer job for the university. Amidst mowing lawns and weeding day lilies, his mind became enflamed with the picture of millions of people behind the Iron Curtain coming to know Christ. The breathtaking encounter with God left him speechless. Due to the dramatic nature of this powerful experience, he revealed it only to me and one other trusted friend. This confirmed what I already knew: I would live my life as the wife of a leader.

God's light from this vision soon guided our lives into the darkness of the Communist world in the midst of the Cold War, where we lived and served for thirty-three years. We raised our family in four different countries with four different languages and four different cultures as a result of such a powerful, God-given vision.

My Current Perspective

Marriage to a man who presses the edge of the envelope exhilarates me, and I acknowledge the privilege of walking arm in arm with a world-changer, where matters of eternal significance permeate our everyday conversations. As partners, Larry and I continue to wrestle with the urgency of getting the Gospel to every man, woman, boy, and girl, to give every person at least one chance to hear the good news that Jesus saves.

However, decades in this arena prove such a life comes with enormous challenges. (Right?) The tsunami of pressure, criticism, long hours, and monster schedules inherent to this calling, requires courage, perseverance, and resilience.

Looking back, I access my journey as a rich and valuable education, though most lessons were not learned with ease. At times, I felt like a lightning rod in the stormy life alongside a leader. Other times, I spoke confidently in public while privately aching from a broken heart. I smiled and shook hands while simultaneously needing someone to hold mine.

Mentored by godly women, I gleaned principles from interviews, books, sessions, and seminars. Most significantly, though, I learned from the Lord. My greatest breakthroughs and life changes emerged from the Word of God in the setting of aloneness with Him. My desperate heart, driven to the Lord day after day, discovered His never-ending resources and His customized care. Blessed by His presence, I continued to move forward in this awe-inspiring life He called me to lead.

My Desire for You

Does any of this strum a familiar chord for you? Do you possess your own version of my friend's dilemma: *What I am supposed to do? What is my contribution?* Have you ever felt that your husband walks around with a target on his back, and you find yourself in the line of fire when the bullets start flying? Do you feel isolated because your husband is their leader, thus friends keep their distance?

Let me ask: Are there times when the only voice you hear is that of the enemy telling you to toss in the towel? If so, please know I understand; I wrote the following pages with you in mind.

I long to see you emerge from these pages exhilarated with how much Jesus loves you, equipped to be the partner He created you to be, and confident that He is sufficient for any situation you face.

Now, let us embark on our shared journey, where we explore four categories of personal growth: Person, Partner, Portrait and Promises. Attention to these categories can transform your effectiveness as a person and as a partner.

Chapter 2

NOT *JUST* MRS. LARRY THOMPSON

BUCKINGHAM PALACE, HERE WE COME!

The summer conference was over, and privileges of the empty nest prevailed. After all, who needed us back at home in Budapest?

Energized by our awareness of freedom, Larry and I emphatically hit the pause button on life, donned our walking shoes, and set out like two newlyweds. An exhibition at Buckingham Palace caught our attention.

In honor of Queen Elizabeth II's eightieth birthday, the Palace offered a rare public viewing—inclusive of a descriptive history—of eighty royal gowns and personal jewelry. Together we toured the spectacular exhibit, and then Larry left for his favorite art museum. I remained behind; I wanted more time to study the gorgeous dresses.

Listening yet again to the audio headset, I gazed at the glitter and glamor, and I read and reread every description provided with each elaborate dress: state dinners, visits with foreign dignitaries, official tours to other nations. As the hour for closing approached, and other tourists slowly exited, I enjoyed the hall all to myself. Only the security guards remained. Wow . . . alone and surrounded by exquisite splendor on display. I yearned to absorb every detail to recall and savor for a lifetime.

Suddenly, in this setting of grandeur and without warning, God intervened with a strong sense of His presence. Amid the soft lights, quiet music, and superb representation of royalty, I heard the strains of Edward Mote's aged hymn play out in my head: "Clothed in His righteousness alone, faultless to stand before His throne."

Debby, your beauty in Christ supersedes all the beauty displayed before you. Nothing compares to the magnificence of your righteousness in Christ. Nothing. Your true identity as My child is royalty, and you are adorned in My garments of salvation, arrayed in holy attire. I stopped. Overwhelmed with wonder, I marveled at the breathtaking encounter. I stood completely still and absorbed this amazing moment with my heavenly Father.

In hushed reverence, my very soul responded with, "Oh God. Thank You. Thank You. You have gently pulled back the curtain for me to see as never before the majesty and privilege of being a child of the King. No other identity compares. I commit myself to growing and living in the fullness of this reality."

My epiphany in Buckingham Palace solidified a conviction: Identity in Christ holds the foundation and the cornerstone for our lives. Everything spiritually, emotionally, experientially, and relationally builds upon it.

In fact, Neil Anderson says, " Understanding your identity in Christ is absolutely essential to your success at living the Christian life. . . . Next to a knowledge of God, a knowledge of who you are is by far the most important truth you can possess."[1] Yet, across the globe, I meet wives of leaders who suffer a common spiritual dysfunction. Though they long to be everything God created them to be, their experience and their desire do not match. A disconnect exists between what they know to be true and what they experience in life.

If you find yourself caught in this dilemma, wonderful news awaits. A strong identity in Christ is available for you, the leader's wife, by implementing three life-changing principles: Believe what is true, reject what is false, choose what will last.

Principle #1: Believe What Is True

You already have Adornments of Royal Identity hanging in your closet:

The Adornment of Significance

Before you ever became a wife, God created you as a person, a marvelous treasure. (Pause a moment and ponder this statement.) Imagine: God created you with a unique personality, character, originality, and distinctiveness. Differentness, singularity, and specialness set you totally apart from all other human beings. Your value to God is incomprehensible.

As a passport describes a person's earthly identity, so the Bible describes one's eternal identity. Psalm 139 emphatically describes your significance:

You are known: "You have searched me, Lord, and you know me. You know when I sit and when I rise; you perceive my thoughts from afar. You discern my going out and my lying down; you are familiar with all my ways. Before a word is on my tongue you, Lord, know it completely. You hem me in behind and before, and you lay your hand upon me" (Psalm 139:1-5).

You were fashioned by God Himself: "For you created my inmost being; you knit me together in my mother's womb. I praise you because I am fearfully and wonderfully made; your works are wonderful, I know that full well. My frame was not hidden from you when I was made in the secret place, when I was woven together in the depths of the earth. Your eyes saw my unformed body; all the days ordained for me were written in your book before one of them came to be" (Psalm 139:13–16).

There is actually a plan for your life: "All the days ordained for me were written in your book before one of them came to be" (Psalm 139:16b).

The Adornment of Security

Never are you alone: "You hem me in behind and before, and you lay your hand upon me. Such knowledge is too wonderful for me, too lofty for me to attain. Where can I go from your Spirit? Where can I flee from your presence? If I go up to the heavens, you are there; if I make my bed in the depths, you are there. If I rise on the wings of the dawn, if I settle on the far side of the sea, even there your hand will guide me, your right hand will hold me fast . . . When I awake, I am still with you" (Psalm 139:5–10, 18b).

The Adornment of Eternal Worth

Your name is written in the Lamb's book of life. When you trusted Jesus Christ as Savior, your name was written in the Lamb's book of life and the entry is extremely personal. In my case, the entry is written not as Mr. and Mrs. Larry Thompson, nor as Mrs. Larry Thompson. No indeed. My name in the Lamb's book of life reads: Deborah Anne Coleman Thompson. Honor, distinction, and eternal worth mark this entry (Luke 10:20; Revelation 21:26). God says in Isaiah 45:4, "I summon you by name and bestow on you a title of honor."

The Adornment of Unconditional Love

God's unconditional love sent His Son to die on the cross as payment for our sins! Cover-to-Cover, the Bible contains verses affirming His love. Jeremiah 31:3 records, "You are loved with an everlasting love."

"The disciple whom Jesus loved" is a description which repeatedly occurs throughout the Gospel of John (see 13:23; 19:26; 20:2; 21:7, 20). Imagine, John chose to personally identify himself with this unique depiction in the Gospel bearing his name. What motivated him to repeatedly make this personal reference?

I believe John experienced, at the core of his identity, the significance of Jesus' unconditional love for him. What about you and me? Are we comfortable describing ourselves this way? If not, what is lacking?

Brennon Manning in *Abba's Child* said, "Define yourself radically as one beloved by God. This is the true self. Every other identity is illusion."[2]

The adornments of royal identity provide a godly wardrobe made of spiritual, emotional, and psychological fabric for us. His desire for us is unshakable security and changeless significance. However, the distance between our head and our heart is enormous.

Let me explain. To know Scripture to be true is simply knowledge. To have Scripture formulate my identity is supernatural transformation. Two of my favorite recipes to prepare are cinnamon rolls and angel biscuits, both of which call for raised dough. I particularly like the experience of working with the dough after adding the yeast. The motion of massaging the ingredients together with my hands gives me a picture of what needs to transpire in my heart. I need to allow God to massage the truth of His Word into the depth of my being so that the knowledge in my head regarding my true identity travels the distance to affect my heart. Then, like John, I need to believe what is true, and identify myself also as the one whom Jesus loves.

Now, we consider the second life-changing principle involved in developing a strong identity in Christ.

Principle #2: Reject What is False

Four False Identities Confront a Leader's Wife.

The Identity Found in Her Husband

The leader's wife may find herself particularly susceptible to defining her identity through the life of her husband. She interprets who she is by her husband's profession, position, status, credentials, and even his income. She makes the devastating mistake of relinquishing her own identity and finding her identity in her husband (in who he is, in what he does, in who he knows, in what he has achieved). This woman, thus, sacrifices the privilege to develop into who God created *her* to be. Over time she becomes so accomplished at living a false identity that she no longer recognizes the true person inside.

Sonya experienced this identity crisis first hand. Her mother's alcoholism robbed her of a university degree. She dropped her studies to work and support the two of them, which resulted in ongoing painful insecurities.

When she and Shawn married, his position on the church staff gave her the long-sought-after security, even significance. His credentials seemed more than sufficient to cover them both. After all, he had two masters and a doctorate. For the first time in her life, she actually felt good about herself. Sonya made the tragic mistake of believing her identity and worth vicariously connected to her husband's achievements.

Now this! Tears blurred the words on the page she tried to hold steady. Someone anonymously slipped this letter with its devastating contents under the door of his office, and Tom held it out for her to read. It stated, "A majority of people feel that, upon receiving this communication, you should resign. The reasons are as follows . . ." The piercing words showed no mercy as she quickly calculated the meaning. Where would this lead?

Such a tragic situation would be difficult for any woman, but especially for the one whose identity is solely found in that of her husband.

The Identity Related to Other Women

The leader's wife may be tempted to define her identity by comparison to other women. In our humanness, we compare ourselves to others, which leads to feelings of inferiority; or we compare others to ourselves, which leads to pride. Both of these comparisons are rooted in self-focus, which is idolatry. Instead of wearing our wardrobe of royal attire, we find ourselves draped in rags of insecurity and insignificance.

The Identity of Her Own Personal Ministry

The leader's wife is vulnerable to seeking her identity through her personal ministry. She measures her worth by ministry success, and equates the affirmation of others as approval from God. A slave to the opinions of others, she suffers addiction to their accolades. Tragically, this woman fails to realize that God's love for her is unconditional and does not depend upon her performance. Desperate to produce results, she relies on her own strength, and fails to rest in grace under the control of the Holy Spirit. Exhaustion and disillusionment confront her at every turn.

The Identity of Her Professional Career

One last category involving false identity remains for us to consider: The leader's wife is tempted to define her identity by her career. This misguided woman has permitted the world with its appealing goals and definition of success to squeeze her into its mold. Driven to achieve professional recognition, her relationship with the Lord and with her husband suffer. Sadly, she is deceived into believing status determines worth.

Principle #3: Choose What Will Last

Does a lasting solution exist for the dissonance between truth and experience? My answer: yes. When we make God's choices our choices, He accomplishes, over time, amazing transformations within our identity.

So, how? How do we move forward to make God's choices our choices?

Model: Choose to Accept God's Model

Determine to make Jesus our model. God never intended for you and me to become like someone else. His divine design intends to make each of us like Jesus. "For those God foreknew he also predestined to be conformed to the image of his Son" (Romans 8:29). John the Baptist understood this truth when he declared, "He must increase, but I must decrease" (John 3:30, NASB). Choosing to pursue God's model sets me free to pursue His best, and enables me to both recognize and reject counterfeits.

Makeover: Choose to Be Transformed

God's amazing makeovers are just that, *amazing*.

We are admonished, "Do not be conformed to this world, but be transformed by the renewing of your mind" (Romans 12:2a, NASB). Our behavior changes when our thinking changes. We begin to act with authenticity, and we are liberated to be who we were meant to be in Christ.

Emma's attendance at a highly publicized women's conference felt awkward. Coerced, she came with a neighbor who promised to babysit later while she Christmas-shopped, if *only* Emma would accompany her to the event. So here she sat.

Emma's appearance portrayed that of a model: young, beautiful, stylish, and always smiling. But the exterior description represented only window dressing. Internally, she was tense, insecure, and fearful. Her performance never seemed worthy enough to cause God to like her. Struggling desperately to earn His approval, she always viewed herself as a failure and a disappointment to Him.

As she listened to the speaker's stories, Emma burst into tears. Trying to juggle her coffee, she reached down into her Louis Vuitton bag on the floor to grab a tissue. Within her, something stirred as never before; the message reached into her deepest longings.

That day, for the first time, Emma saw a glimpse of Jesus' eyes smiling at her and actually *delighting* in her. Desperately she wanted to believe its truth.

Could it be real that Jesus is wild about her, even on her worst day—that He doesn't want her performance? Was the speaker correct in saying He wants us in humility to accept His love, flowing from His grace, not only for our salvation, but also for our sanctification? These riveting words spoke a message of hope for her.

Her Christian home upbringing emphasized behavior rather than heart. Admittedly, she was doing the same thing with her own children. Listening with fixed focus, Emma's perspective of herself and her relationship with Jesus underwent a radical transformation. The takeaway was astounding: *Jesus delighted in her.*

To experience the truth and transformation Emma discovered, allow me to recommend two practical steps.

Monitor Your Self-Talk

Listen to your own voice inside your head. When you make a mistake, when you fail, what message plays in your thinking? This disciplined awareness yields positive change. Determine to say to yourself what God says about you. In a short time, you can experience incredible changes by taking control of your mental thought process.

I urge you to meditate on particular Bible verses. Go a step further and own them. Develop a personal arsenal for counterattack. John 8:32—"You will know the truth, and the truth will set you free"—along with Romans 8:1—"Therefore, there is now no condemnation for those who are in Christ Jesus"—are two of my favorites.

Allow me to share the story of a dear friend who painfully suffered from insecurity. When we first met, she rarely made eye contact. Always gazing down at her shoes, she only muttered muffled attempts at conversation.

Her thinking underwent radical transformation regarding who she is in Christ, and today she appears like a lovely flower, which gracefully opened under the light of the love of God. Her personal presence speaks volumes about His power. Furthermore, her ministry to women has grown by leaps and bounds, because within herself she discovered life as a new creation in Christ (1 Corinthians 5:17).

Make Your Focus the Wardrobe That Will Never Wear Out

Have you ever considered the Bible as a fashion magazine? Actually, we possess the best issue ever written, both in the Old and New Testaments. Read below to discover what I mean.

"I delight greatly in the Lord; my soul rejoices in my God, for he has clothed me with garments of salvation and arrayed me in a robe of righteousness" (Isaiah 61:10a).

"Clothe yourselves with the Lord Jesus Christ" (Romans 13:14a).

"Clothe yourselves with compassion, kindness, humility, gentleness and patience" (Colossians 3:12b).

Focusing on our spiritual wardrobe highlights amazing garments, garments which are customized and comfortable. Without fear of ever being inappropriately dressed, we own the best attire for every occasion. Most importantly, this attire always draws attention to our Beloved Designer. Now tell me, what woman wants to turn that down?

Maintaining a dual identity is stressful, demanding, confusing, and tense. I learned this firsthand during The Cold War when we lived covertly as missionaries behind the Iron Curtain. Thus, I urge you to let God synchronize your head and your heart to enable you to live out your true identity in Christ. He does not need another actress.[*]

Identity in Christ, a rare and beautiful treasure, must be vigilantly guarded to protect against identity theft. The closer we grow to Jesus, the more we experience who we really are, and the easier it becomes to detect and reject the fakes and frauds within ourselves. Building on this foundation is the cornerstone of a vibrant personal walk with Christ.

Be who God meant you to be, and you will set the world on fire.

– Saint Catherine of Sienna

---

[*] Author Terry Blaylock

Living with Eternal Intentionality™

"May [you] have power . . . to grasp how wide and long and high and deep is the love of Christ, and to know this love that surpasses knowledge" (Ephesians 3:18-19a).

Does your view of yourself align with God's view of you? If not, where is there need for change?

God fashioned you as a person, a marvelous treasure, prior to your ever becoming a wife. When you became a follower of Jesus, your name was written in the Lamb's book of life. How does this reality make a difference in your self-perception?

What incorrect thought pattern poses your biggest challenge in believing the truth that God loves you and delights in you?

Which of the Four False Identities threatens your true identity? What change is needed in order to enable you to live according to your true identity?

Significance, security, eternal worth, and unconditional love are your inherited adornments as a child of God. What is one step you desire to take to clothe yourself in these royal garments?

Please pray aloud in a quiet aloneness with your heavenly Father: Thank You, God, that You created me. Thank You that because Jesus died for me, my name is written in the Lamb's book of life. I want to define myself as a woman radically loved by You. Enable me to release any part of my identity that is not my true self in You. Please make me the person You created me to be.

Cameo

Katherine von Bora

1499-1552

The following glimpse into Katherine's life is gleaned from *Great Women of the Christian Faith* by Edith Deen.[3] Katherine von Bora lived out her true identity in Christ. Born January 29, 1499, in Lippendorf, Germany, she entered the convent at age nine. It seemed she would spend her life there and her identity would be that of a nun. The Reformation changed not only her eternal identity, but it also changed the course of her life. She became a true follower of Jesus and married the courageous reformer, Martin Luther. He was forty-two, and she was twenty-five. Would the marriage last? "History records that the marriage not only succeeded, but set a high standard for Christian family life for centuries to come."[4]

Katherine cared for her prestigious husband and the bustling household while also ministering to the needs of people all over Wittenberg, where they lived. She listened to their problems, gave them care and medicine in their sicknesses, counseled them in their sorrows, and advised them in their business affairs. The town recognized that the Luther household was an exemplary Christian home, and much of that success was due to Katherine.

"Martin Luther was generally cheerful and had faith in his God, yet occasionally he became moody. At such times, Katherine sought to comfort and encourage him. Once, when nothing seemed to raise Luther's spirits, he decided to leave home for a few days to see if a change would help him, but he returned grieved in spirit.

On entering the house, he found his wife seated in the middle of the room, dressed in black, with a black cloth thrown over her head, and looking quite sad. A white handkerchief she held in her hand was damp, as if moistened with tears.

When Luther urged his wife to tell him what was the matter, she replied, 'Only think, my dear doctor, the Lord in Heaven is dead; and this is the cause of my grief.'

He laughed and said, 'It is true, dear Kate; I am acting as if there was no God in Heaven.'" Luther's melancholy left him.

None of her [Katherine's] many sorrows was greater than the loss of her husband in 1546, twenty-one years after their marriage. He had gone to his native town of Eisleben in Saxony to settle disputes between the quarreling counts of Mansfield. Having suffered from ill health for ten years, he was not equal to the severe winter he had to endure there.

Katherine's deep affection for her husband is expressed in this letter which she wrote to her sister soon after his death:

> "Who would not be sorrowful and mourn for so noble a man as my dear lord, who served not only a single land, but the whole world? If I had a principality and an empire, it would never have cost me so much pain to lose them as I have now that our dear Lord God has taken from me, and not from me only, but from the whole world, this dear and precious man."

For new strength, Katherine Luther turned to Psalm 31: "In thee, O Lord, do I put my trust; . . . deliver me in thy righteousness . . . be thou my strong rock . . ." (vv. 1-2, KJV).

In 1552, the bubonic plague spread over Wittenberg, and the university was moved to Torgau. Katherine decided to seek refuge in this town to which she had journeyed to safety as a nun almost thirty years earlier. En route, the horses pulling the carriage in which she and her four children were riding became frightened. Anxious for her children's safety, she jumped out of the fast-moving vehicle and tried to stop the horses, but she fell into a ditch of water. This experience was too much for her gallant spirit. She soon developed bronchial trouble and for several months lay ill, comforting and sustaining herself by praying. She died on December 20, 1552, and joined her husband in their eternal heavenly home.

Katherine von Bora Luther left her indelible mark on history. "She represented the new spirit of the Reformation, and played no small role in transferring the ideal of Christian service from the cloister to the home."

Chapter 3

LONGING FOR A BURNING HEART

MIA PULLED INTO THE COFFEE shop after dropping her children off at school. Fatigue threatened to suffocate her, and she desperately needed the caffeine to work a miracle. A bad morning, yet another in a string of bad mornings, colored her outlook. The baby cried off and on through the night, making it difficult to crawl out of bed when the alarm blared. Ethan was on another one of his many trips, and she felt wasted.

At the breakfast table, complaints of wrinkled school uniforms from the older children greeted her. Their grumbling about cold cereal complicated the morning milieu. After all, how was she supposed to be cheerful, energetic, and productive when she faced these ongoing mornings alone?

Then the phone call added pressure to the tense morning. The nurse at her doctor's office informed her she needed to return for a retake on her mammogram.

Only a brief eighteen months earlier, her sister lost the battle with breast cancer, and the raw pain still hurt unmercifully. Of course, the needed appointment made her wonder, "Am I next?"

Broken sleep, backbreaking fatigue, bad news, and bills created quite a list. She still smarted from the embarrassing episode yesterday at the grocery checkout line: card denied.

Sitting here sipping the rich brown liquid, Mia fantasized about a harmonious home, a healthy body, and a happy marriage. The nagging question haunted her: How much longer could she go on? Her life felt like a boat approaching Niagara Falls, and she feared impending disaster. Did some secret exist to decode life?

Come to Me, all you who are weary and burdened, and I will give you rest.

Where did that come from? Mia blocked out the music and conversation around her to allow the ancient life-giving words to speak to her soul and penetrate her current reality. Maybe there was a secret; maybe this was it. *Come to Me . . .*

Yes, a secret to life does exist; the secret lies within an intimate relationship with Jesus. From personal experience, I speak not of program or plan, rather of passion—a passion for an intimate relationship with Jesus. Such a relationship with Jesus awaits any woman, even those with daunting situations like Mia's, who is willing to invest in the pursuit of intimacy, which involves intentionality, time, and trust.

Listen above the roar and clamor of life to the clarion call from Jeremiah 30:21: "Who is he who will devote himself to be close to me?" An intimate relationship with Jesus for a leader's wife involves devotion to three passions: a passion to worship Him, a passion to walk with Him, and a passion to withhold nothing from Him.

A Passion to Worship Him

Choosing to spend time alone with Jesus stands as our greatest privilege and highest priority. With the dawning of every new day the invitation recurs, "Let the one who is thirsty come; and let the one who wishes take the free gift of the water of life" (Revelation 22:17b). You and I are invited to join with "thousands upon thousands of angels in joyful assembly . . . and worship God acceptably with reverence and awe" (Hebrews 12:22, 28). This daily celebration provides a magnificent opportunity to enjoy God.

However, this heavenly invitation competes for an RSVP. Late nights, laundry, lunches, headaches, errands, appointments, problems, and people clamor loudly for our attention. How can we be expected to silence the roar and sit still in the presence of God? Is this pursuit even humanly possible in our frenzied, media-dominated generation?

The answer rests in the word **choice**. And, this dilemma is not confined to the twenty-first century. Consider the plight of two sisters in Luke 10:38-42.

Faced with identical circumstances, they each must individually **choose**: *sit with Jesus or serve Jesus*. Mary **chooses** to sit at the feet of Jesus, listening to Him, hanging on every word. Martha, however, chooses otherwise. Distracted and anxious, she opts out of this blessing.

Jesus' gentle admonition for Martha instructs you and me: "Martha, Martha, . . . you are worried and upset about many things, but few things are needed—or indeed only one. Mary has **chosen** what is better, and it will not be taken away from her" (Luke 10:41-42, emphasis mine).

Life has taught me two secrets for success. These secrets work hand in hand and happen almost simultaneously. I do not always get it right, but when I do, the day is definitely different.

Secret Number 1: *Morning moments are disproportionately potent.*

The first nanoseconds of wakefulness set the tone and trajectory for my entire day. This tentative, fragile, sensitive, vulnerable zone is *pivotal*. Mentally managing these moments is a secret of success.

Secret Number 2: *Gratitude is the game changer.*

Armed with intentionality, I must choose to take ownership of my attitude, and direct the needle of my internal compass towards gratefulness. My "Daily Doxology" is one deliberate step I have learned to take. Before Facebook, before text and Twitter, before ESPN—*even before my devotions*—it is essential for me to articulate to God that I am grateful. It is not complicated, but it is clear. My road map for right direction goes like this:

Lord,

Thank You that the sun came up.

Thank You for the seasons.

Thank You for my Savior.

Thank You that my sins are forgiven.

Thank You for the Spirit who lives within.

Thank You for sanctification.

Thank You that I am set free from my sins.

Thank You for a supernatural marriage.

Thank You for sweet family relationships.

Thank You for significant friendships.

Thank You for the Scriptures.

Thank You that I am a sojourner.

Thank You that springs of living water flow from my innermost being.

Thank You that my eternal destiny is secure.

Thank You for a set-apart purpose in life.

Thank You for supporters and their faithfulness.

Thank You that You are sovereign.

Thank You for the joy of starting new endeavors.

Thank You for small groups, places to connect in community.

Thank You for such adorable grandchildren.

Grateful people are happy people. The descriptive message from Psalm 68:3 is to die for! "May the righteous be glad and rejoice before God; may they be happy and joyful." These framed words sit front and center in the foyer of our home. *But these words do not come into being by accident or osmosis.* These words come to life for the one willing to intentionally manage the morning.

Yes, mornings matter. And, intimacy flows morning after morning as I start the day with intentionality to worship Him. No short cuts, no fast formulas, just day after day meeting alone with Jesus to worship Him. My Bible, my journal, and my coffee are my companions.

Though I believe this with every fiber of my being, I still need ongoing motivation. In the cover of my Bible I have written for myself the words from Isaiah 50:4b: "He wakens me morning by morning, wakens my ear to listen like one being instructed." This reminder serves to promote my commitment to this awesome, life-changing opportunity, to send an affirmative RSVP to God Himself.

A Passion to Walk with Him

"Satisfy us in the morning with your unfailing love, that we may sing for joy and be glad all our days" (Psalm 90:14). Now we walk across the bridge of connectivity, walking from our private worship with Him into our public day with Him.

Walk by the Spirit (Galatians 5:16)

(Respond firmly but patiently to the child who whines about the food you have prepared.)

Walk in the way of love (Ephesians 5:2)

(Be gracious to the grouchy neighbor.)

Walk in the light (1 John 1:7)

(Resist the urge in your ladies' Bible study to share negatively about your husband.)

Walk in obedience to His commands (2 John 1:6)

(When tempted to worry about your bills, turn to prayer.)

Moreover, walking with Christ involves discovering His preplanned priorities.

Are you surprised to discover that God possesses a plan, an agenda for your day? At first, I was. But give thought to Ephesians 2:10:

"For we are God's handiwork, created in Christ Jesus to do good works, which God prepared in advance for us to do."

Amazing. My busy day takes on incredible significance when I actively engage with Him regarding my to-do list. As I allow Him to be my Personal Life Coach and guide me, a supernatural productivity results. This approach to time management makes even the mundane meaningful when His priorities become my priorities, and deep, lasting satisfaction results. I need only to ask.

To walk with Jesus means moving forward one step at a time, by His side, in the power of the Holy Spirit, day in and day out, holding His hand, not pulling away. He sets the pace, He marks the path, and He chooses the course. Somewhere along the way, ever so imperceptibly, I am startled to realize that a deeper intimacy has transpired.

I speak not of a philosophy, a code of ethics, an ideology, or a creed, but a God-centeredness that consumes the totality of our lives. Acts 17:28 is one of my cherished verses: "In Him we live and move and have our being."

Intimacy flows from intentionality to walk with Him. A vibrant, intimate relationship with Jesus takes time, yet the reality occurs as we walk and talk along the road of life. I ache for the intimate joy of a burning heart that never loses its fire of love for My Savior. The last few verses of the Gospel of Luke explain this life-long pursuit of mine.

"Were not our hearts burning within us while he talked with us on the road and opened the Scriptures to us?" (Luke 24:32).

Walk with me through a story from our lives in Europe.

A walk? "Would you like to go on a walk together?" As the church service ended, Walt and Pat Stuart approached us and extended the invitation; Larry and I eagerly accepted.

On this brilliant fall Sunday afternoon, the four of us set out. Newly introduced, we relished the opportunity to get better acquainted. Ours was no ordinary walk—this was a *Wanderweg*.

Jogs, sprints, and marathons each have their place, but the European *Wanderweg* holds a category all its own. I speak of walking for the sheer joy of walking; steady, rambling walking for the delight of the company you keep. (I miss it sorely).

Our *Wanderweg* with Walt and Pat consumed the entire afternoon. Through the orchards, around the cows, near the sheep, we walked. Breathtaking, pastoral scenes, resplendent with fall foliage, unfolded before us in magnificent display.

Whether walking in pairs or walking single file, we just kept talking—ours was a rolling meandering dialogue, just like our surrounding rolling meandering terrain. Various personal stories moved with us as we steadily moved forward—stories of families, dreams for our future, and passion for our common Christ-calling. Conversation, contemplation, even commiseration composed the fabric of discussion.

We stopped at a *Gasthaus* for rich brown coffee and authentic Black Forest torte. This pausa marked our midpoint; the *Wanderweg* took us back home. Our foursome set out in the warmth of sunshine; we returned at a chilly dusk.

Reflections stayed with me from our classic *Wanderweg*, which started with an intentional invitation.

Peaceful—The experience was overwhelmingly bathed in peace.

Purposeful—The focus was relational, getting to know each other.

Pace—The one-step-at-a-time trek moved us forward with deliberation, but this was not a race against the clock.

Pauses—The pauses were as significant as the progress; we stopped at appropriate intervals to reflect, to ruminate.

And, it is no wonder . . . I still pause when I read: "Enoch walked with God" (Genesis 5:24a, NASB).

Enoch. Walked. With. God. That must have been quite the *Wanderweg*.

A passion to worship Him and a passion to walk with Him lead to:

A Passion to Withhold Nothing from Him

Fear. For years fear described my relationship with God. I became a follower of Christ at an early age, and I knew heaven as my eternal destination.

Yet, the issue of control existed between God and me. I trembled at the thought of His plan for my life, fearing He would send me to Africa as a missionary. Afraid to release my grip on my own destiny, I relentlessly wrestled with God. This paralyzing fear not only dominated my relationship with Him, spiritual panic attacks occurred.

As a university student, in a dormitory bathroom the course of my life changed forever. One afternoon, exhausted from the battle, I knelt on the cold hard floor and prayed:

"God, I give up; I let go. I am tired of being afraid of You and Your plan for my life. I release, one tight finger at a time, the fist of control on my life. My palms are opened up; here, I am offering my life out of my hands into Yours. I finally realize if You loved me enough to send Your Son to die on the cross to pay for my sins, then You love me enough to provide what is best for me. I will do anything You want me to do; I will go anywhere You want me to go, even if it means Africa as a missionary."

With my utterance of *Amen*, I collapsed, weak with relief. Before I even got up off my knees from the tile floor in Hathorn Hall at

Mississippi State University, heaven itself flooded my heart with peace. The contrast was so extreme I desired never to return to my former way of life, that of a fear-based relationship with God.

When my fingers start to tense around anything (and they do) I sense a heart tug by the Holy Spirit—Hathorn Hall, the bathroom, the ultimate life contract. Let go. Release this situation into the loving hands of your heavenly Father.

Intimacy with Jesus depends on a passion to withhold nothing from Him. Intimacy thrives within absolute trust.

But we never can prove the delights of His love

Until all on the altar we lay;

For the favor He shows, for the joy He bestows,

Are for them who will trust and obey.

These words penned in 1887 by John H. Sammis are absolutely true; I know.

Living with Eternal Intentionality™

"Satisfy us in the morning with your unfailing love, that we may sing for joy and be glad all our days" (Psalm 90:14).

When was the last time you sat quietly and heard Jesus say to you, "Come to Me all you who are weary and burdened, and I will give you rest"?

If the secret to life is an intimate relationship with Jesus, how can your mornings be reconfigured to reflect the pursuit of this intimacy?

By way of gratitude, the game changer, take a moment and write your own "Daily Doxology."

Is there an aspect of your life that you are clutching to control? Define what is needed for you to release this to Jesus and exchange it for His peace?

"Grant us always to know that to walk with Jesus makes other interests a shadow and a dream."

– Valley of Vision[5]

Cameo

Elisabeth Elliot

1926-2015

"NO!" I screamed.

Reality showed no mercy. The impersonal screen of my iPhone delivered the news that my dear friend and beloved mentor Elisabeth Elliot was with Jesus. Over the last decade, I attempted to prepare myself for this moment. Not even close. My world was now a world without her, and of all things, I learned this on Facebook. No warning, no cushion, and no "I'm sorry I have to tell you this . . . "

I immediately dialed Elisabeth's number at Strawberry Cove. Aware of a deep ache inside of me, I wanted desperately to talk to Lars, her husband of 38 years; I wanted to hear his rich, velvety voice. He would provide the personal touch missing from a cold, social media announcement.

No, again. The answering machine clicked and waited for my message. Pain and emptiness were gaining a foothold here, and I needed to be alone with God.

Climbing the three flights of stairs to my corner office in our Athletes in Action® headquarters, I stared out the window at the lovely grounds below. Sunshine and beautiful flowers met my gaze—beauty in my bereavement.

Gone. With only the silence to distract me, I prayed, "Oh God, I worship You. I worship You for the incredible ministry she had in my life."

I sat down, and I began to remember.

Elisabeth was one remarkable lady. I met her publicly, and then grew to know her privately. What an unspeakable privilege to have known her as my mentor and as my friend.

Soft-spoken and precise, she never wavered when it came to the choice of obedience to the Lord. No, she was not a saint, but she was certainly set apart to mark a generation with her wholehearted devotion to Christ.

I experienced her clarity mixed with kindness over our first shared meal. She and Lars had flown to Garmisch, Germany, where she was a guest speaker for our annual Eastern European Women's Conference. As conference coordinator, I made sure to take advantage of the opportunity to reserve a private meal with her. A quiet table in a European restaurant marked our sweet beginning. Over dinner, surrounded by a cacophony of noises, I ventured to ask, "May I call you Elisabeth?" There was no mistaking her answer, "Yes, but thank you for asking." Whew.

Now that we were on a first-name basis, the real question weighing heavily on the soul of this young wife of a leader tumbled out. I suddenly became remarkably vulnerable with a woman I had just met. *What do you do with criticism of your husband?* Without batting an eye, she went straight to the point with precisely the answer I needed to hear.

"Well. First of all, certainly no one likes it." Shock. Had I heard her correctly? Heaven and earth stood still as my soul came up for air.

No being made to feel guilty for struggling.

No quick-fix verse.

No vague spiritual airs.

No sermon or suggestion.

Just a true, forthright transparency. "No one likes it." With that response we bonded; a treasured friendship was birthed. Elisabeth and I launched into a lifetime that would leave me forever changed by her wisdom and uncommon understanding.

Honestly, I was not prepared to like her so much. But a single answer from her changed my life. I immediately knew that I could trust her; I could learn from her; I could really like her.

Over *Apfelstrudel* and coffee, I listened intently as she shed more divine light on my painful question. "Remember, God has given him a grace to bear this criticism. You do not have the same grace that he has, but God has given him grace for the criticism. Also, remember, there is probably a grain of truth within the criticism that he needs to hear. Allow God to use this in your husband's life."

Repeatedly, I have returned to the teaching at a table at the foot of the Alps, instruction that truly changed my life. Thank You, God; thank you, Elisabeth. In the coming years, I would turn to her with countless other questions. The story was always the same—unconditional acceptance and grace-filled wisdom.

I remember her gentleness with our children. As we visited on other hallowed occasions around our dining room table, she treated them as if they were her own grandchildren. Their questions were handled with tenderness and respect. I smile while reflecting on the discussions.

"What was your favorite animal when you lived in the jungle?"

"The toucan."

"Why do you use one name with your books and another with your husband, Mr. Gren?"

"When you are a writer, it is important that your readers who knew you in the past can trust you to be the same person in the present. You don't want to confuse them with different names."

"What was the strangest thing you ever ate in the jungle?"

"Monkey!"

Laughter followed, of course.

Elisabeth and I would go on to journey together in the coming years, mostly at a distance, but our lives intersected when geography allowed. She remained consistent: uncompromising obedience, crystal clear clarity.

Once in Budapest, as we sat drinking apple juice and eating cookies, she offered much-needed advice, "Don't worry. When I think back on my life and consider the things I worried about, I realize it was a colossal waste of time. And keep a quiet heart."

I miss her. One day, in The Land That Is Fairer Than Day, at The Marriage Feast of the Lamb, we will enjoy far more than *Apfelstrudel* and coffee.

Elisabeth modeled courageous faith. Her wisdom was gleaned from her experiences as a twice-widowed wife, mother, grandmother, missionary, Bible translator, radio broadcaster, public speaker, and best-selling author. Her many books include *Keep a Quiet Heart, A Path Through Suffering, The Savage My Kinsman,* and *The Shadow of the Almighty.*

Elisabeth Howard was born in Brussels, Belgium, where her parents served as missionaries. She graduated from Wheaton College and later went to Ecuador as a missionary. In 1953, she married a former classmate, Jim Elliot. Together they worked on translating the New Testament into the language of the Quichua Indians. Their daughter, Valerie, was born in 1955. Ten months later in 1956, Jim was killed by the Auca Indians while attempting to take the Gospel to that primitive tribe. Elisabeth continued her work among the Quichuas, and she later lived and worked among the Aucas.

She returned to the United States and remarried. Her second husband, Addison Leitch, a professor at Gordon-Conwell Theological Seminary, died of cancer in 1973. Elisabeth remarried, and until her death, she lived north of Boston, Massachusetts, with her husband, Lars Gren.

Of her own spiritual journey, Elisabeth writes, "At the age of ten, I wanted to be born again. It was very simple. I took God at His word, 'received' Him, and was given the power to become a child of His."

Gateway to Joy[6] contains significant spiritual lessons, which have been transferred from Elisabeth's pen to my heart:

Set aside time for God.

It is a good and necessary thing to set aside time for God in each day. The busier the day, the more indispensable is the quiet period for prayer, Bible reading, and silent listening. It often happens, however, that I [Elisabeth] find my mind so full of earthly matters that it seems I have gotten up early in vain and have wasted three-fourths of the time so dearly bought (I do love my sleep!). But I have come to believe that the act of the will required to arrange time for God may be an offering to Him. As such He accepts, and what would otherwise be "loss" to me I count as "gain" for Christ. Let us not be "weary in well-doing," or discouraged in the pursuit of holiness. Let us, like Moses, go to the Rock of Horeb, and God says to us what He said to him, "You will find me waiting for you there" (Exodus 17:6, NEB). *(A Lamp for My Feet)*

Do not be afraid to tell Him exactly how you feel.

He's already read your thoughts anyway. Don't tell the whole world. God can take it—others can't. *(Keep a Quiet Heart)*

Let Him redeem it.

Are you sure your problems baffle the One who since the world began has been bringing flowers from hard thorns? Your thorns are a different story, are they? You have been brought to a place of self-despair, nothingness. It is hard even to think of any good reason for going on. You live in most unfavorable conditions, with intractable people, you are up against impossible odds. Is this something new? The people of Israel were up against impossible odds when they found themselves between the chariots of Egypt and the Red Sea. Their God is our God. The God of Israel and the God of . . . thorns looks down on us with love and says, "Nothing has happened to you which is not common to all. I can manage it. Trust Me."

He wants to transform every form of human suffering into something glorious. He can redeem it. He can bring life out of death . . . .When our souls lie barren in a winter which seems hopeless and endless, God has not abandoned us. His work goes on. He asks our acceptance of the painful process and our trust that HE will indeed give resurrection life. *(A Path Through Suffering)*

Pray for your husband.

Lord, grant me the vision of a true lover as I look at _____. Help me to see him through Your eyes, to read the thoughts he does not put into words, to bear with his human imperfections, remembering that he bears with mine and that You are at work in both of us. Thank You, Lord, for this man, Your carefully chosen gift to me, and for the high privilege of being heirs together of the grace of life. Help me to make it as easy and pleasant as I possibly can for him to do Your will. *(Newsletter)*

The life of Elisabeth Elliot has been a living example of the prayer of missionary Bette Scott Stamm, a prayer that, at sixteen, Elisabeth copied in the back of her Bible.

"Lord, I give up all my own plans and purposes, all my own desires and hopes, and accept Thy will for my life. I give myself, my life, my all, utterly to Thee to be Thine forever. Fill me and seal me with Thy Holy Spirit. Use me as Thou wilt, send me where Thou wilt, work out Thy whole will in my life at any cost, now and forever." *(These Strange Ashes)*

Elisabeth left this life with the same exactitude with which she had lived it; at 6:15 a.m. on 6-15-15 she departed. Imagine that.

Chapter 4

GROWTH IS FOR GROWN-UPS

THE HONKING HORN ANNOUNCED A fresh episode. Everyone else— already in the car—waited on this teenager. All the way to church I would be reminded how my habitual tardiness affected the rest of the family. I would be told that we were destined to walk in "just like the McBride's," the notorious family that predictably paraded in, single file, long after the service began. (Never mind that they lived closest, just across the street.)

So, with rollers still in my hair and makeup in my hand, I tumbled into my backseat position, and sought to create some semblance of decency out of the product of my tardiness. This was no fun. After all, who wants to be called "the cow's tail" even if the illustration merits consideration?

Since that season of life, my teenage habits have undergone renovation, yet I remain time-challenged. Rarely will I ever be the first to arrive at a meeting. There will still be the occasional mad race to the airport. The Big Clock App will perpetually be needed on my iPhone. I will always be glad when you are not early to my front door.

I promise promptness for The Rapture or for my own funeral, depending on which comes first. However, between now and then, I must constantly be vigilant to arrive where I am going with punctuality. Bottom line: I must tenaciously pursue growth.

Self-awareness, personal assessment, and the desire for change provide stepping-stones to discovering God's customized plan for personal growth. Entering partnership with Him for spiritual formation within one's strengths, weaknesses, flaws, and limitations leads to an exciting new future of hope and broader horizons of influence.

Perhaps punctuality is not your battle, yet we each face personal deficiencies, gaps where breakthroughs are needed. To be the women God created us to be, you and I must seriously embrace the ongoing need for development. Growth involves change and often produces pain. However, growth in character, integrity, and personal maturity mold us more and more into the likeness of God's Son.

John Henderson, an expert in leadership development, teaches that the single greatest factor to determine my ongoing maturity is *me*. A program cannot overcome a lack of personal ownership of the passion and motivation to excel still more in my own personal journey of being transformed into the image of Jesus Christ.

"Spiritual maturity is one of the greatest needs in the church today . . . After over a quarter of a century of ministry I am convinced that spiritual immaturity is the number one problem in our churches. Not everyone who grows old grows up. There is a difference between age and maturity."[7]

These sobering words from Warren Wiersbe, author and Bible teacher, challenge us to place a high priority on personal growth. Such an attitude will embrace maturation as an ongoing life value.

The answers to four questions offer pathways to personal growth in Christ. I suggest we consider them separately.

1. What is growth?

Growth is the godly, intentional pursuit of Christ-likeness. This spiritual dynamic takes place when we grant the Holy Spirit access to every area of our lives. The healthy spiritual process of maturation aids you and me in individually becoming the person God designed. He involves people; He incorporates community to move us toward His desired outcome: our looking and living like Jesus.

Meet my friend Candice, vibrant, fun loving, and loyal. Like a valuable antique, our relationship is a classic, which has stood the test of time (and geography). Multiple times, trains, trunks, boxes, suitcases, and moving vans have transported both our families across the globe, and in different directions. Thankfully, our friendship has managed to survive the transitions.

Whenever possible, Candice and I relish the opportunity for a visit. Picking up right where we last left off, she and I launch headlong into heart-to-heart sharing.

On this particular evening, she and I sat for one of our marathon dinners. When I sensed the gravity of her topic, I put down my fork and gave her 100% focus.

"I am overwhelmed at a recent occurrence God brought about in my life. Recently, while sitting at a traffic light, I turned my head and noticed a sad sight; a poor woman walked down the sidewalk pushing a grocery cart.

"Since this was not an area of poverty, her presence stood in stark contrast to her surroundings. Though I pitied her, I pulled away when the light changed and distanced myself from the sight of the poor woman. At least I thought I did.

"Into the next few blocks, the Holy Spirit began speaking to me. He made it clear that I was to stop, interrupt my busy day, turn around, and go back to that woman. Sensing that the Lord offered no option for me to wiggle out of, I returned, parked my car, and located the woman who had by now rested on a bench.

"Without fanfare, I pulled out several bills and offered them to her. She looked up at me and said, 'I didn't ask you for money.' 'I know,' I said, 'but the Lord told me to give it to you. In the name of Jesus I offer you this.' She hesitantly pulled her hand from her ragged coat pocket, and took the cash. I smiled at her, turned, and walked away. Though I regularly drive past that bench, I have never seen her again."

I sensed that Candice was not done. After pausing to take a swallow of water, she continued.

"I am so excited to share this story with you, Debby, because the episode was totally from the Lord. This was so unlike me. I don't consider myself to be very compassionate, and normally I wouldn't have taken the time to be bothered about such a woman."

With tears Candice said, "I truly see Jesus working in my life, softening my heart, and making me more compassionate. I am so excited to see that He is changing me."

What a story! This incredible example lifted from the pages of life, displays ongoing growth in Christ.

God longs to make us more like Jesus. His Son is His best blueprint, and He desires for you and me to look and act like Christ. "For those God foreknew He also predestined to be conformed to the image of His Son" (Romans 8:29a).

Peter points his readers toward the model of Jesus when he writes, "Grow in the grace and knowledge of our Lord and Savior Jesus Christ" (2 Peter 3:18a).

The Bible paints a beautiful word picture of growth. "Blessed is the one who trusts in the Lord, whose confidence is in him. They will be like a tree planted by the water that sends out its roots by the stream. It does not fear when heat comes; its leaves are always green. It has no worries in a year of drought and never fails to bear fruit" (Jeremiah 17:7-8). This vivid, fruitful imagery indicates growth in Christ, as revealed in Candice's life.

2. What enhances growth?

In a world with steroids and Miracle-Gro, do quick-growth enhancers exist for the Christian life? No. Growth, a very personal component in our relationship with God, involves a right attitude, and a right appetite.

First, there needs to be a right attitude of humility. My heart needs to be humble before God and admit that He alone can make me the person He created me to be. Furthermore, I must acquire an appetite that hungers and thirsts for righteousness. This spiritual appetite for right living is characterized by Bible reading and prayer on a daily basis. The Holy Spirit acts as our coach and personal trainer to take what we invest in and supernaturally empower us to grow in Christ-likeness. Beyond this, time is essential for growth to occur. I am convinced that when we walk in the light of His Word, in the power of the Holy Spirit, over time, transformation will take place.

Environmental factors often provide a catalyst for growth. Christ-honoring churches, small group studies, and seminars and books certainly contribute.

However, saintly lives of persecuted believers show us that none of these are prerequisites to growth. Some of the godliest people I know grew spiritually *in spite of* conditions that could be labeled as spiritually deprived. Because of their attitude of humility before God and their hunger for Him, they demonstrated a quality of growth that was, humanly speaking, unexplainable.

God does His amazing work to develop us into Christ-likeness in spite of our circumstances—or in light of our circumstances—when we place our attitudes and appetites into His Hands.

Intentional goals, ongoing feedback, a personal development plan, and a godly friend provide invaluable resources for growth. Renée has been such a friend for me. As a peer mentor, she has walked with me through needed areas of growth in my own life, and she consistently points me toward Christ.

One particular aspect of my life and leadership needed attention—group dynamics. After meetings where we both attended, Renée and I would later engage in a debrief session. Over steaming cups of tea, we shared heart to heart about my most recent interaction. Confident of her love for me, I respected her observations.

At times, she affirmed my participation. On occasion, she offered corrective feedback. This trusting relationship contributed to my growth in Christ, and my effectiveness as a leader.

Let me ask: Do you have a Renée in your life? If not, petition God to help you locate her. Your growth, like mine, will thrive. You will be astounded at the change as you overcome weaknesses that perhaps plagued you for your entire life.

3. What inhibits growth?

A short list of hindrances to growth includes fear of change, a self-sufficient attitude, indifference, insecurity, and busyness. However, sin is the all-time, greatest block to growth. Just this morning I keenly sensed an awareness of my own sin. Allow me to explain.

Confidentiality stands out as a tremendous value to me, and I consider this a personal strength. That is, until this morning.

I feel so crummy; my actions in a situation lacked discernment, and the ramifications hurt individuals closest to me. Considering my options for damage control, the temptation arose to simply cover up the matter and move on. After all, why create more confusion? I rationalized this as the quickest, easiest, and most efficient way to move forward.

Then the Holy Spirit brought to mind Psalm 51:6: "You desire truth in the innermost being" (NASB). A choice loomed: Do God's right thing and leave the consequences with God, or create my own solution. Thankfully, I concluded the only way forward required transparency with God and transparency with these beloved individuals.

I took a deep breath, prayed, and made the phone call. My words were, "I was wrong; I am sorry; will you please forgive me?" Sin threatened to block growth in my own life, and bruise the relationships involved. Easy? No. Right? Yes. Growth stands as too priceless to allow sin to impede the process.

Allow me to ask: Is there a roadblock in your life right now which impedes your growth in Christ? If so, what action does the Lord desire you to take? Maybe, like me, you need to make a phone call. Maybe, you need to make a visit. Whatever it is, take the needed action. Your growth in Christ is worthy of the initiative.

A second boulder to spiritual growth revolves around secondhand Christianity. Again, a personal story comes to mind.

Standing at the stove, I turned and looked out the window. Mindlessly, I studied the snow and listened to the familiar hum. The music of the microwave told me my coffee was being reheated, warmed over. It was no longer fresh, and it needed to be reheated. The end of the morning came before the need for caffeine abated. My coffee would be drinkable—but not fresh. The product of the microwave would be doable, but not delightful. Reheated. And quick.

Hmmm . . . This reminds me of another word—recycled.

I became a pupil in the classroom of recycling when we lived in Germany. Hand it to the Germans; in the early 1980s, this nation took the lead and established itself on the cutting edge of the global recycling movement. They successfully (operative word being successfully) trained an entire nation in the nuances of recycling.

Back then, as domestic-in-chief, I bought in, and as a household, we participated—thoroughly. Red bins for this, yellow bins for that, and green bins for the other. On ski slopes, in schools, in cities, in villages, recycling was rampant. And I marshaled our troops to march to the recycling beat.

Now in America, I watch—and participate—as our nation learns to become a nation of recyclers.

However, there is yet another arena where we face reheated and recycled. Follow me here.

Spiritually speaking, large portions of our diet with God and His Word can subtly come to us reheated and recycled. By this, I mean we take what another has learned, and we make it a disproportionate share of our diet. Though this is appropriate, appreciated, and certainly has its place, this is no substitute for fresh and first. Fresh and first are discovered in time alone with God—just the two of us. I listen firsthand to God; I learn firsthand from God.

What I glean is fresh, not reheated—first, not recycled. Fresh and first remove the third party, eliminating someone in between God and me.

Not reheated: warming over what someone else learned and reheated to serve me. Not recycled: what someone else says that God said.

Granted, the reheat-recycle approach for our spiritual nutrition is tempting, since it is fast and convenient. But I believe our souls are starving for fresh and first.

Truthfully, the pursuit of intimacy with Jesus behooves us to pursue fresh and first, requiring time and planning. And longing . . . Matthew 5:6 tells us, "Blessed are those who hunger and thirst for righteousness for they will be filled."

What is growth? (becoming more Christ-like)

What enhances growth? (right attitude, right heart)

And what inhibits growth? (sin and secondhand Christianity)

This brings us to one final question.

4. What must I do to grow?

Red Alert! Be aware: this incorporates perseverance, not perfection, sanctification, not sinlessness.

The Bible speaks of growth, not perfection. An ocean of difference separates the two. A perfectionist harbors a subtle form of pride. Human perfection is both an idol and a phantom. Only Jesus was perfect, and when my goal is perfection, His place of preeminence is challenged. I will be perfect only when I see Him face to face. Until then, He wants me to pursue Christ-likeness, to seek to grow to be like Him, not like a picture of perfection that is a figment of my imagination.

A fast-track growth plan guaranteed to prosper comes out of the Book of Hebrews (12:1-2). The title of the plan: Lighten up, look up.

Lighten up: "Let us throw off everything that hinders and the sin that so easily entangles. And let us run with **perseverance** [not *perfection*] the race marked out for us" (12:1b, emphasis and comment mine).

I envision a backpack chock-full of debilitating weight (performance, petty comparison, perfectionism)—hindrances and sin leaving you worn out and exhausted. And true growth mandates lightening the load. So, toss aside everything that hinders, toss aside the burdensome weight of sin dragging you down.

Look up: Then, fix your eyes on Jesus (12:2). He is the Author and Perfecter of your faith. By looking at Him we become more like Him. Remember? That has been God's plan all along, "For those God foreknew he also predestined to be conformed to the image of his Son" (Romans 8:29a).

So go! Get rid of the weight and get on with the race. Run lighthearted and free! And enjoy the magnificent, life-giving journey of growth. From time to time, take a look in the mirror—you are looking more and more like Jesus.

Living with Eternal Intentionality™

"Grow in the grace and knowledge *of our Lord* and *Savior Jesus Christ. To* him be glory both now and forever! Amen" (2 Peter 3:18, emphasis mine).

What are your thoughts regarding the teaching of John Henderson who said, "The single greatest factor to determine my ongoing maturity is *me.* A program cannot overcome a lack of personal ownership of the passion and motivation to excel still more in my own personal journey of being transformed into the image of Jesus Christ"?

Is there a matter in your life right now, which is blocking your growth in Christ? If so, what action (a phone call or a visit) is the Lord leading you to take?

What one idea will you implement to insure *fresh and first* (not reheated and recycled) describes your walk with Jesus?

Has your growth been sidetracked by seeking perfection rather than focusing on perseverance? If so, how will a change in focus set you free to embark on the life-giving journey of growth?

Cameo

Ruth Graham

1920-2007

Many reporters ask me who is the greatest Christian I have ever known. I always answer, Ruth.

– Billy Graham

Ruth Bell Graham's life (June 10, 1920–June 14, 2007) was an inspiring journey of faith and love. Ruth modeled growth in Christ in an extraordinary way, and as a writer, poet, wife, and mother, she was a powerful presence in the life of her husband, Billy Graham.

Born in China, Ruth Bell was the daughter of medical missionaries, where her father, Dr. Nelson Bell, served as a surgeon. One of four children, Ruth was brought up with a Christian faith that would shape her life. She stated, "Not only did Mother and Daddy teach the faith in the home, they lived it. And as a consequence it was easy as a child to give my heart to the Lord Jesus."

Ruth Bell came to the United States to attend Wheaton College in suburban Chicago. Traveling aboard the *USS McKinley*, contemplating her avowed spinster existence, she penned these now prophetic words: "If I marry, he must be so tall when he is on his knees, as one has said, he reaches all the way to heaven. His shoulders must be broad enough to bear the burden of a family. His lips must be strong enough to smile, firm enough to say no, and tender enough to kiss. His love must be so deep that it takes its stand in Christ and so wide that it takes in the whole world. He must be big enough to be gentle and great enough to be thoughtful. His arms must be strong enough to carry a little child."

When she met her future husband he quickly made an indelible impression. "I heard him praying and I thought, 'There is a man who knows to whom he is speaking.' I remember getting on my knees that night and just saying, 'Lord, if You will let me spend the rest of my life serving You with him, I will consider it the greatest privilege.' I didn't know at the time what that would imply."

Ruth and Billy were married in 1943 in the North Carolina mountains. The young couple soon returned to Illinois where Billy became pastor of a small church in the Chicago area. He later served as a traveling evangelist with a new organization called Youth for Christ. In 1949, he began a ministry that would eventually reach millions. Ruth had a profound influence on his message, and was an indispensable partner as the Graham ministry grew.

By the late 1950s, the Grahams had five children and a permanent home on a mountaintop near the North Carolina village of Montreat. Ruth's responsibility as a mother was demanding. Often when Billy was away at crusades, she was on her own to raise three daughters and two sons as her husband traveled around the world with his message of salvation through Jesus Christ. Saying good-bye, often for months at a time, was never easy. Ruth's faith helped her face these trying times: "Looking back on my life, I thank God for especially the tough times. That's when the Bible comes to life for you. That's when the Lord Jesus becomes the most real to you." After their children were grown, Ruth often joined her husband on the road, where she frequently shared her faith with others.

Ruth's ministry as a writer began to flourish in the 1980s. She would author several books of spiritual insight and poetry. In 1996, Ruth and Billy Graham became only the third couple in U.S. history to receive the Congressional Gold Medal. With nineteen grandchildren, dozens of great grandchildren, and friends and admirers around the world, Ruth Graham's life was filled with blessings. Her warm heart and her gracious spirit were the hallmarks of a ministry that will endure.

In her later years, Ruth said, "I've enjoyed growing old. There is so much to look forward to after this life. And so much to look back on. And the thing that stands out in my life, above everything else, is the promises of God that you have seen come true."[8]

Oh, time! be slow!

it was a dawn ago

I was a child

Dreaming of being grown;

A noon ago

I was

With children of my own;

And now

It's afternoon

And late,

And they are grown

And gone.

Time, wait!

– Ruth Bell Graham, 1974[9]

Partner

Chapter 5

A ROCK STAR REINTRODUCED

MEET SUSIE, A LEADER'S WIFE and a mother of four. Pregnant and facing brain surgery in less than 48 hours for a malignant tumor, she posted the following on her website:

> Being pregnant and having a brain tumor makes you kind of famous. I've gotten quite a bit of attention lately, which has been at times funny, embarrassing, heartwarming, and always humbling that so many people are praying for us. I mean—SO MANY people—all around the world. The verse that keeps coming to mind is from Proverbs 31, where in talking about that elusive "ideal" woman, it says, "She laughs at the days to come." Most of Proverbs 31 . . . well, we might say it "lies outside of my giftedness," (ha!) but what a gift God has given me—the ability to laugh. Obviously, I'm not laughing because I don't think this is serious or because I'm arrogant enough to think that the future can't hold bad news. But, there is a lot to laugh about. And, ultimately, a craniotomy can't take from me what is most important.[10]

With a dramatic glimpse into her own life, Susie referenced a leader's wife from Scripture that God brought into my life more than forty years ago.

To be honest, initially I found this ancient woman from the Bible unpleasant. I misjudged her as being obsessed and performance driven, so I kept my distance. Over time, God gently reintroduced us. Now, I see her differently and value her greatly. At long last, I appreciate her—not her performance—but her person. Join me in becoming acquainted (or reacquainted) with this leader's wife (v. 23) from long ago as we read in Proverbs 31.

10 A wife of noble character who can find? She is worth far more than rubies. 11 Her husband has full confidence in her and lacks nothing of value. 12 She brings him good, not harm, all the days of her life. 13 She selects wool and flax and works with eager hands. 14 She is like the merchant ships, bringing her food from afar. 15 She gets up while it is still night; she provides food for her family and portions for her female servants. 16 She considers a field and buys it; out of her earnings she plants a vineyard. 17 She sets about her work vigorously; her arms are strong for her tasks. 18 She sees that her trading is profitable, and her lamp does not go out at night. 19 In her hand she holds the distaff and grasps the spindle with her fingers. 20 She opens her arms to the poor and extends her hands to the needy. 21 When it snows, she has no fear for her household; for all of them are clothed in scarlet. 22 She makes coverings for her bed; she is clothed in fine linen and purple. 23 Her husband is respected at the city gate, where he takes his seat among the elders of the land. 24 She makes linen garments and sells them, and supplies the merchants with sashes. 25 She is clothed with strength and dignity; she can laugh at the days to come. 26 She speaks with wisdom, and faithful instruction is on her tongue. 27 She watches over the affairs of her household and does not eat the bread of idleness. 28 Her children arise and call her blessed; her husband also, and he praises her: 29 "Many women do noble things, but you surpass them all." 30 Charm is deceptive, and beauty is fleeting; but a woman who fears the LORD is to be praised. 31 Honor her for all that her hands have done, and let her works bring her praise at the city gate.

This leader's wife is a rock star! Consider her character qualities articulated in the verses we just read: wise, kind, compassionate, trustworthy, energetic, organized, successful, enterprising, positive, even likable. A pleasure to be around, she accomplishes volumes. Bottom line: kind and competent.

Commonalities with a twenty-first century woman jump out at us. Part of a dual income family, she works outside the home, and sustains incredible demands on her time. Without a mobile phone or a computer, she demonstrates expertise at networking.

A community-minded humanitarian, she portrays life lived with intentionality and authenticity. In spite of pressure, she does not whine about the future, and she still manages to squeeze in fitness training. Whoa.

This amazing person possesses a wide bandwidth. Without a doubt, she operates in her sweet spot. But how? What explanation exists for her success? Most of all, what is her secret? By looking into this inspiring life, we observe three dynamic examples, which equip her as a partner with no guilt and no regrets.

Example #1: She is a Woman of Faith

One thing! Out of one thing comes everything. Let your finger travel down the text to verse thirty where four words decode her life: "She fears the Lord." This is it! Her strength of character, her wise counsel, her domestic engineering, her relationship with her husband all flow from one choice; her worship, her reverent awe of the Lord.

A vibrancy and authenticity point to her devotion to God which permeates her relationships and her priorities. Her relationship with the Lord oozes authenticity as she moves in and out of the lives of people around her.

Our friend models the quintessential example of faith in action. For her, being a woman of faith is an authentic way of life. Because of her Biblical worldview, she serves as an ambassador for His kingdom.

Jesus beckons you and me, as His followers, to integrate His love into all levels of society. Our eternal destiny is lived out on the stage of daily life before a watching world. The Great Commission is our holy homework assignment, and every believer is commissioned in the military of our Master (Matthew 28:18-20).

In Acts 1:8, we see a progression of thoughtful participation: "But you will receive power when the Holy Spirit comes on you; and you will be my witnesses in Jerusalem, and in all Judea and Samaria, and to the ends of the earth."

In living with eternal intentionality, I suggest Jerusalem represents our home, our family, those God has entrusted to our care. Judea and Samaria perhaps means the neighborhood, or the homeless shelter across town. And "the ends of the earth" may literally mean going to the ends of the earth, as in my situation. For another, this perhaps leads to participating on a mission board at one's church, or serving from home on one's computer as an online missionary to reach people with the Gospel.

This offering of participation shifts through the age and stage of family life with the Lord and in counsel with one's husband. God always guides when we pray, *Lord, You know my life situation and my constraints. With the portion of discretionary time You have given me, how and where do You want me to make a contribution in helping to reach my world with Your glorious Gospel? Where do you want to use me as your Great Commission Christian?*

When we grasp the profound significance of our mission, every detail of every activity takes on new meaning. When faced with requests for involvement, we say *yes* with conviction, and *no* with confidence. Strategic living from conviction, motivation, and eternal intentionality disarms guilt and regret.

Choosing to live as women of faith (not as a label, but as a lifestyle), you and I also discover the sweet spots for which God created us. Set free from the desperate attempt to do everything, we are empowered to do anything He places upon our hearts and in our paths to do.

Example #2: She is a Woman of Character

At the core of our Proverbs woman of faith, her character creates a formidable foundation. Here we observe this impact in her speech and in her outlook.

Speech

Simply put, when she speaks she has something worthwhile to say, and she says it kindly. An uncomfortable reality emerges. A leader's wife must live without a common luxury, the luxury of careless speech. Others place a disproportionate perspective on our opinions and remarks. Thus, tolerating our own indifference to our comments, our criticisms, and our language is not an option. (*Ouch.*)

Think further with me regarding our habits of speech. Trash talk often takes its toll while driving to church, first thing in the morning, last thing at night, right before guests walk in, right after guests leave, right before entering as guests, right before a major ministry event, or right before departing for a ministry trip. Out one side of our mouths we can praise a neighbor for bringing over a meal, and out the other side of our mouths lambaste our husband for not taking out the garbage.

James says that this ought not to be. We feel uneasy when we read, "With the tongue we praise our Lord and Father, and with it we curse human beings, who have been made in God's likeness. Out of the same mouth come praise and cursing . . . this should not be. Can both fresh water and salt water flow from the same spring?" (James 3:9–11).

So therefore, are we hopeless? Quite the contrary.

Hope exists for life-giving words to become a way of life. First, we make this an internal issue, rather than a surface issue. I believe with all my heart the answer lies within the heart.

Our words are birthed in our hearts, not in our mouths. "Above all else, guard your heart, for everything you do flows from it" (Proverbs 4:23). Our hearts operate as the formation factory for our words. Transformation in speech results from the renovation of hearts.

And secondly, slow down. You ask, "How can that make any difference?" A life-giving communication pattern that works comes also from the writings of James: "Everyone should be quick to listen, slow to speak and slow to become angry" (James 1:19b).

Before you ever utter a word, give the Holy Spirit a nanosecond to get ahead of you and pave the way for godly communication. Impetuousness blocks Him. So, I repeat, slow down, yield to Him, and *watch your conversation become full of grace, seasoned with salt, so that you may know how to answer everyone* (see Colossians 4:6). Our Divine Orator displays His glorious grace when we get it right in what we say.

Outlook

She smiles at the future. Our Proverbs 31 mentor further influences our lives as we consider this uncommon approach to life. I believe she smiles at the future because she lives with an eternal perspective. To know with confidence that God inhabits my future frees me from anxiety today. What an enormous contribution to bring to a partnership of life with a leader.

In my last semester at university, this verse became my anchor: "She smiles at the future" (31:25b, NASB).

Upon graduation I planned to become a staff member of Cru® (formerly known in the United States as Campus Crusade for Christ®) and move away. Walking into my future with God meant walking away from Larry, the love of my life. As a sophomore in university, he would remain on campus as a student for two more years. The pain of embarking on an unknown future without him gripped my heart and challenged me emotionally.

Tempted daily by fear of the unknown, the innocent discovery of these words (while sitting on my dorm bed and quietly reading my Bible) charted an entirely new course for me. The Holy Spirit used the Scripture to calm my growing anxiety, and give me a sense of joy regarding my upcoming departure. I realized my future held a direct connection to the character of God, not to my circumstances, my location, or even my proximity to Larry. Using His Word, God tenderly spoke to my heart during those final university days, *I am already residing there in your future. You need not fear.*

Over the decades, I have repeatedly returned to this truth for comfort when worry about life ahead—the future—threatened to consume me.

A feeling of dread set in when, as a young married couple, we approached a challenging move to our Cru assignment in New England. Being pregnant, this transition meant our first baby would be born in Massachusetts, not in Mississippi. Without family nearby, without familiarity of medical community, this same verse again provided solace and emboldened my wavering heart.

Only a year later, Proverbs 31:25 accompanied me in saying good-bye to our precious families in 1977 before boarding the plane to fly into the great unknown and live covertly behind the Iron Curtain. *Trust Me with your unknown future, Debby. I am already there, waiting for you, with My open loving arms.*

As we moved forward to follow God's unique call on our lives, we often encountered the question, "How could you?"

How could you leave your parents and take their only grandchild to live so far away in an unsafe, unknown Communist-controlled country?

Over the years, I tried in multiple ways to answer the question posed by others. I would reply from all angles—answer of logic, answer of emotion, answer of reason. Each had its audience. I gave the Biblical perspective, the spiritual perspective, the godly perspective. Countless times the response I received in return was a blank stare, a grimace, sometimes even a glare.

In spite of my attempts to communicate, I did not possess within my human self an answer. Never did I have an explanation, save one, that landed truthfully: *the will of God.*

God made His call on our lives to go to live covertly behind the Iron Curtain so unmistakably clear that to refuse to go would have been willful, blatant disobedience.

However, the domino effect of our decision left gaping holes in the hearts of those we left behind. Their sorrow was genuine, and their pain ran deep. At the outset, close friends of theirs offered strong opinions. One predicted Communist prison for us. Another suggested my parents phone Washington and blow our cover. In the face of these challenges, I found myself helpless to *fix it*. Constantly, I had to put my own heartache into the holy hands of God.

Sorting clothes, stuffing luggage, and finalizing travel arrangements were like objects on an emotional conveyor belt moving us toward our inevitable separation. Watching my mother tearfully kiss our 17-month-old goodbye and seeing my daddy turn his head away took my soul to depths it had never before plumbed. Hugs . . . tears . . . and one last look punctuated our parting. My strength to let go and move forward with hope came from three truths anchored in the Word of God, enabling me to smile at the future.

God's will is good, acceptable, and perfect (Romans 12:2b). Hard does not mean wrong.

God's will is consistent; His will for me was also His will for my parents.

God's will is ultimately the safest place on earth to be, even when His will meant living a covert, undercover life as a missionary in a Communist nation.

For you and me, our leader-husbands live forward with their God-given dreams and visions. Our temptation in walking with them—to fear the unknown future—is real. Thus, God graciously provides these words: "She smiles at the future." We lean into this extraordinary verse from our extraordinary God as we lean into this extraordinary life.

Example #3: She is Woman of Trust

"Her husband has full confidence in her . . . She brings him good, not harm, all the days of her life" (31:11-12). A final look at the profile of our friend in Proverbs 31 reveals a timeless, invaluable trait: trust. She's got her husband's back.

Private life and public productivity operate in a potent connectivity for a leader. A man finds it impossible to concentrate on the demands of leadership while possessing a mind clouded by trouble and tension at home.

Any leader would attest to this truth. A wife holds enormous power and influence over her husband and his effectiveness as a leader. The quality and tenor of their relationship either puts wind in his sails or holes in his hull.

This behooves you and me to seek God's supernatural strength to send our leader-husbands to the city gates without baggage from breakfast. With intentionality, in relying on the resources of the Holy Spirit, we demonstrate camaraderie for who he is and what he does. Trust serves as a confidence builder throughout his busy day, and forms an unseen fabric for productivity. All is well away from home when all is well back at home.

Let us review.

The leader's wife in Proverbs 31 portrays a life characterized by supernatural qualities, for only God's power creates such a person. He fashioned this woman to be godly, wise, kind, compassionate, and trustworthy because of her life commitment to Him.

With reverence and worship of God as our bedrock foundation for who we are and what we do, a vibrant supernatural quality of life results. Our character, our words, our relationships, and our marriages bring glory to Him and blessing to our world.

May we return often to reflect on this passage, which describes this unknown wife of a leader. Don't you agree, she's quite a girl? I encourage you to embrace her priorities of faith, character, and trust as your own priorities. In so doing, over time, you will be well on your way to becoming the partner God created you to be.

Do you realize:

She is never defined as the perfect wife; she just makes the perfect choice. She fears the Lord (verse 30).

She could be anybody.

She is not even given a name. We are not told who she is, but Whose she is. She lets that one thing affect everything.

Living with Eternal Intentionality™

"Teach us to number our days that we may present to You a heart of wisdom" (Psalm 90:12, NASB).

What is this woman's outstanding secret? How does her bedrock foundation serve to guide you in planning your own priorities?

What do you learn from her speech (Proverbs 31:26) and from her outlook (Proverbs 31:25b)? How can these observations positively influence your own life?

Where has God currently called you to serve Him as a Great Commission Christian—in your Jerusalem, Judea, Samaria, or the uttermost part of the earth (Acts 1:8)?

In your situation, describe what life looks like when you have your husband's back (Proverbs 31:11a, 12).

Cameo

Vonette Bright

1926-2015

A dry, merciless, desert heat defined the day. A mysterious wind accentuated the intensity of the temperature. As I walked the pebble path, the weather and my nervousness walked with me.

My classes were over for the day, and I headed toward a small bungalow on the property of Arrowhead Springs. The appointed afternoon finally arrived for my visit with Vonette, the wife of Bill Bright.

Currently at the headquarters of Campus Crusade for Christ® (as Cru® was known then) in Southern California, I immersed myself in training to join this movement. Yet, too often my heart drifted across the country back to Mississippi; deeply in love, I sorely missed the one I loved. He worked as a summer youth director at a small church in a small Southern town, and our lives stood worlds apart.

As I walked, I wondered, "What would Mrs. Bright be like?" I had heard her speak, but that was at a distance when she stood behind a podium. What would it be like to be with her, one-on-one, in her home?

With embarrassment, I recall requesting a private appointment with a woman I had never met, an extremely busy woman with endless demands on her schedule. But I was driven by love. As the wife of a great spiritual leader, I wanted her answer for the largest question on my heart.

For this occasion, I carefully selected a short-sleeved cotton dress with a round Peter Pan style collar. I can still picture the black, orange, white, and green tiny floral print. The wide, elastic waist made it comfortable. (Candidly speaking, that dress was too short—much too short. Blame it on the 1970s. Good thing this was California).

Upon reaching the top of the path, the red tile roof of their bungalow home came into view. I navigated my way downward, crossed the courtyard, and rang the doorbell. While I waited, a lizard scurried past. At least one detail felt familiar to Mississippi.

A smiling Mrs. Bright welcomed me and invited me to take a seat in her lovely living room. I moved toward an aqua velvet chair while she returned to her kitchen to retrieve two glasses of a cold beverage. In this moment alone, I admired the numerous gifts on display from around the world, and desperately attempted to quell my nervousness.

Momentarily, Mrs. Bright rejoined me in the matching pair of chairs; I could tell this meeting was important to my hostess. Concurrently, I sensed the need to get to the point, so I swallowed a gulp and launched.

"I came, Vonette, to ask you a question about a young man in my life. We love each other, and I need your input. So, my question is this: What can I do to best prepare myself for my relationship with him?"

Gripped with love, I possessed no better sense than to bring this dreamy question to this leading woman in the evangelical world, this question of my aching, longing, love-smitten heart.

Without blinking she asked, "Honey, are you engaged?," as if engagement would make a difference in her answer.

Embarrassed, I sheepishly responded, "Noooo. No, we are not engaged." Pause. "But there is a real possibility for a future together." (I surely didn't tell Larry of my answer to her!)

Sitting in her pale, pastel-colored living room, she answered, and there was nothing pale about her advice.

"Honey, you just get to know Jesus. That is the best thing you can do in your relationship with this young man."

Looking back on that hot day at Arrowhead Springs in 1972, I am so glad Vonette knew—not what I wanted—but what I needed. Her Spirit-anointed answer seemed way too simple and far too short.

I secretly longed for romantic suggestions. I came to her hoping for a curriculum, a list of books to read, a guaranteed formula for becoming the woman I wanted to be. I anticipated far more than I received, at least that is what it seemed.

"Honey, you just get to know Jesus."

Even now, I marvel at the lasting impact of her words, for what was true then is still 1,000% true today. The one best thing I can do for my relationship with Larry remains to get to know and *keep* getting to know Jesus.

Imagine: One hot afternoon. One young woman. One short sentence. One lifetime lesson. Thank you, Vonette. Your words have born lasting fruit. I commit to continue sharing your wisdom with other young naive women, who like me, yearn to live life to the fullest alongside dynamic leaders as we partner to help fulfill the Great Commission.

A contemporary model of Proverbs 31, Vonette, along with her husband, Bill Bright, cofounded Cru®. She authored or co-authored more than twenty books and numerous Bible studies and devotionals. The founder of The Great Commission Prayer Crusade, Vonette enjoyed being a mother and a grandmother.

I always appreciated her forthright ability to articulate her commitment to her leader-husband.

Once, when I asked her, "What does it mean to you, Vonette, to be the wife of a leader?," she responded by saying, "Honey, come here. Let's sit down."

We pulled away from the center of the party and made our way to a couch in the corner where she began to talk. Her thoughts flowed as one who spoke from the voice of experience and the voice of conviction. I felt privileged to hear this woman's answer.

"Get ready to share him with other people, lots of other people. You must be ready to do this. This requires you to think and have a plan, and be aware of his situation. You will find yourself getting jealous, but don't be jealous. Be as involved as you possibly can in his world. Other women will be in his world. But you be the first to do what he needs done, if at all possible. Be actively involved with him.

"My first calling is to be the wife of Bill Bright. I would say *no* to anything that he did not want me to do. Go where he goes, be in his world. Pursue what he is involved in," she said. "I chose to have no other field for myself. I would ask myself, what does he need? And then I would seek to meet that need."

When asked, "What was your job description on staff with Campus Crusade for Christ?" she responded with conviction, "To be the wife of Bill Bright. I just looked for what needed to be done, and I tried to do it."

Chapter 6

PLAYING DOUBLES

LOUISA LOOKED IN THE MIRROR and fought back an avalanche of tears. Would anyone even recognize her tonight? Getting dressed for her highschool class reunion was painful. Being pregnant, yet again, took a toll on her appearance, that's for sure. If anyone probed with questions, she feared an emotional collapse. Not living the life she dreamed, combined with the anguish of attending this event, had her in shambles already.

Her old clique assumed she shared their excitement in being together. Hardly the case. She felt left out and worse still, left behind. How long before they perceived her anguish? Would they detect her disillusionment with her marriage that she fought so viciously to hide?

Michael seemed to be a leader in his profession—if that's what you called it—but she never managed to gain traction in his world. This reality confronted them every day, as predictably as the rising of the sun. She even considered leaving and returning to her parents, to this very room where she now stood. But once the children came, and they came quickly, she acknowledged her parents were no longer an option.

When she tried to figure out what went wrong, she got lost in the details. Yes, she loved God. Yes, she considered herself a follower of Christ. She could even say that she loved Michael. After all, he was a wonderful husband and a terrific father. They had a decent income, which allowed her to hire a sitter and invest in her online photography course.

So why this nagging, free-floating anxiety?

If totally honest, Louisa would have to say that she just wasn't committed to the life she and Michael were leading. Being the wife of an executive pastor was more than she bargained for. Perhaps she and Michael should have discussed the demands of this profession more thoroughly before they married. "I just assumed it would all work itself out, this desire of his to be in ministry. If I had only known then what I know now."

Was there hope for their marriage? Did a midcourse correction exist to save her (and them) from shipwreck?

Louisa is not alone. Around the world, I meet wives who struggle to find their bearings alongside their leader-husbands. A vague sense of dissatisfaction surfaces as the common thread. Initially, they assume life after marriage works itself out, but when reality sets in, these assumptions run out of gas.

A marriage partnership offers a rich, fruitful, satisfying reality when one makes the decision to drive a stake into two pledges: a pledge to a divine covenant and a pledge to a shared life. These personal pledges provide the bedrock spiritual antidote for both protection and peace.

I invite you to join me as we delve into this concept of a marriage partnership.

A Pledge to a Divine Covenant

Consider a divine covenant between you and God to embrace three words: acknowledge, accept, agree.

I *acknowledge* it is God's will for my husband to be anointed with the spiritual gift of leadership. I welcome this as a blessing, and as God's divine plan for our marriage. In being called to him, I am called to this. We lead and serve together, with him at the helm.

I *accept* God's call on his life to be both holy and hard. I am not simply resigned to this reality; I genuinely accept it. Acceptance frees me to recognize that it is God's design in creating my husband as a leader. The decision for his leadership gifting is God's choice. Our lives will not be the same as the lives of friends, neighbors, other family members, or coworkers. Ours will be different—not better, but different.

Being married to a leader is an invigorating, stimulating experience. The uniqueness of this calling brings with it a uniqueness of challenges. My greatest challenge will be to pull *with* God's design, not against it. I humbly realize that ours is no ordinary life. I accept that I will need to share my husband with large numbers of people, that schedules will be long and demanding, that spiritual battles will be more intense on our family and our marriage. I must be vigilant and spiritually prepared. Stress, pressures, and expectations will be enormous, but I believe *His divine power has given me everything I need for a godly life through my knowledge of Him who called me by His own glory and goodness* (see 2 Peter 1:3).

I agree to bring a spirit of humility and wholehearted participation to this divine partnership, for God's glory and our good. My vision for stewardship of our partnership embraces the mission to further the Kingdom of God. *I will not cherish exaggerated ideas of myself or my importance* (see Romans 12:3).

I recognize this to be:

God's will—from God.

God's call—of God.

God's glory—for God.

After reading and rereading the words above, I suggest setting apart a time alone with God where you prayerfully make this pledge to Him. *In acceptance lies peace.*

- Elizabeth Elliot

A Pledge to a Shared Life

Shared life does not mean same life—absolutely not. Perhaps God placed you in a venue of service different from your husband's. In such a situation, a pledge to a shared life, still reflects a conscious decision to play on your husband's team mentally and emotionally.

Once you agree with God (divine covenant) that your husband is living a life of obedient service to Him as a leader, I urge you to embrace this life (shared life) wholeheartedly. Choose to believe that God's will is good, acceptable, and perfect (Romans 12:2b, NASB). Eliminate thinking that the grass is greener on the other side of the fence, the other side of the street, or even the other side of town.

Be his "First Lady" and walk side by side. Put yourself philosophically alongside your husband, and view the world of leadership together. Pull with him—not against him—as you embrace God's design for your lives, which is both a privilege and a responsibility.

In your innermost spirit, determine not to be:

A silent partner

A controlling partner

A whining partner

A partner who walks ahead

A partner who walks behind

Rather, as you participate in this life calling, choose to be an asset and not a liability. Fight against the temptation to be aloof, indifferent, distant, or disengaged. Your gifting, your insight, and your expertise are invaluable to this partnership, and it is incomplete without you. Rejoice that you have the privilege to be *both* who you are and where you are.

The Holy Spirit provides our only resource to make this design a reality. Yielding to Him moment by moment for His filling and empowering makes possible God's supernatural provision for you and me. He promises to fill, to enable, and to abundantly bless us in seeking to live life as the partners He created us to be.

In my own life, intersections of faith and future collided along the way and challenged my commitment to a shared life. Episodes occurred when my actions failed to communicate 100% loyalty.

Travel with me to revisit my covert life behind the Iron Curtain. Our son and second child, David, was born in 1979 in a Communist-run hospital in Warsaw, Poland. Soon after, in 1980, we welcomed our second daughter, Grace, to our family. (Our first child, a daughter, was Anne Coleman.) All the while, Cold War tensions escalated and global threats challenged our determination to stay at our assignment. We felt caught between Washington, D.C., and the Kremlin, democracy and Communism. With goods and services rationed and shortages ever increasing, our future seemed to hang in the balance.

A godly colleague of ours and trusted teammate offered this advice: "Under these dire circumstances, it makes complete sense for you all not to reside here. The grave food shortages and political tensions present insurmountable challenges for a family."

This global crisis placed our marriage in its own predicament. Larry and I found ourselves caught in a place of agony heretofore not experienced as we struggled to determine what this meant for our family.

From my perspective, I deduced that our tenure of residence behind the Iron Curtain would end. I was *SURE* that God would not require us to continue to raise our family under such restrictions. Soviet troops were massing at the border. Polish factory workers were repeatedly going on strike. Students were staging "sit ins." A military conflict seemed inevitable, and the thought that we, as citizens of a NATO country, would be found living behind enemy lines made my blood run cold.

I combed the Bible and mined Scripture to validate my position. Using Numbers 32:1-33, I approached Larry with a well-organized Bible study and logical system of thought. This passage records the dilemma where the two tribes of Israel reason with Joshua that they should stay on the east side of the Jordan River while the other ten tribes went in to claim the Promised Land.

I presented my application of the passage to my husband with deep conviction: God's will for us, like the two tribes, meant we should reside in Vienna in the zone of safety, rather than live in Warsaw with the political and economic crisis. Convinced of this Biblical explanation for my position, I pled with Larry for us to relocate and not reside within the confines of a hostile assignment.

Larry, after lovingly listening to me and treating my concerns with great seriousness, took a day alone with the Lord in prayer and fasting to seek His leading for our future. Hour by hour I waited and prayed earnestly for him to see God's will from my vantage point.

At the end of this watershed day, he returned with this conviction:

"Debby, God's call on our lives has not changed. The Lord's will for us does not include relocation." Upon hearing his words, my commitment to a shared life hung in the balance. Yet in the quietness of my disappointment, I knew he was right. Though difficult to hear, the truth rang clear.

As I considered my response (whether or not to trust in Larry's leadership in discerning God's leading), the ancient words of Jeremiah 6:16 tenderly whispered the message my soul needed to hear: "This is what the Lord says: 'Stand at the crossroads and look; ask for the ancient paths, ask where the good way is, and walk in it, and you will find rest for your souls.'"

Somewhere, alone in a European café, I latched on to the glorious promise gleaned from the Old Testament: "My Presence will go with you, and I will give you rest" (Exodus 33:14b).

God's incredible love and supernatural peace—even *rest for my soul*—accompanied this monumental decision. Some of the sweetest days in the life of our family, and some of the most prolific days in our ministry followed as we continued to live and operate covertly behind the Iron Curtain.

I readily share the conviction gleaned from our challenge: The safest and most blessed place to be is in the center of God's will, even when this means living in the capital of a Communist-controlled country with the threat of a military takeover.

A pledge to a divine covenant and a pledge to a shared life will look differently in each marriage; however, the pillars represent a determination on your part to play doubles regardless of the challenges in the game.

Living with Eternal Intentionality™

"Trust in the Lord with all your heart, and lean not on your own understanding; in all your ways acknowledge Him, and He shall direct your paths" (Proverbs 3:5-6, NKJV).

Which of these two challenges do you find more difficult:

a. Acknowledging it is God's will for your husband to be anointed with the spiritual gift of leadership?

b. Accepting that God's call on his life (which directly affects your life) is both holy and hard?

How will you choose to trust God in making changes to your viewpoint related to the previous question?

In your own words, explain why a shared life does not mean the same life.

Do you see yourself as being on your husband's team? If not, what would represent a positive adjustment?

How do you pull with your husband—not against him—in accepting God's design for your lives?

Cameo

Abigail Adams

1744-1818

"Abigail Adams holds the distinction of being the first Second Lady and the second First Lady of the newly birthed United States of America."[11] The scholarly work, *John Adams* by David McCullough, brings this extraordinary woman and her extraordinary marriage to life. The following glimpse into Abigail's life is gleaned from his work.

Born into the family of a minister, Abigail Smith had two sisters and one brother. Considered too frail for school, she was taught at home by her mother. With Reverend Smith's library of several hundred books at her fingertips, Abigail became an avid reader and lover of poetry. Intelligence and wit shone in her, and she was consistently cheerful. Her thirst for knowledge prepared her to live alongside a man who was a lawyer, a member of the Continental Congress, an appointee to the Courts of France and England, Vice President, and then President of the United States of America.

"Miss Adorable," as he referred to her in private correspondence, and John Adams were married by her father on October 25, 1764. Her mother objected to the marriage, but the determination of both John and Abigail and their attraction to each other—like steel to a magnet, John said—were more than enough to carry the day.

His marriage to Abigail was the most important decision of John Adam's life. She was in all respects his equal, and the part she was to play would be greater than he could possibly have imagined. Her determination that he play his part in history was quite as strong as his. They were of one and the same spirit. [She urged,] "You cannot be, I know, nor do I wish to see you, an inactive spectator . . . We have too many high-sounding words, and too few actions that correspond with them."

Extremely long separations of months, even years, characterized their fifty-four years of marriage. Written correspondences sustained their relationship through these prolonged absences and today are treasured artifacts. From them we learn how heavily John Adams relied on his wife. She was the ballast he had wanted, the vital center of a new and better life. To no one was he more devoted. She was his "Dearest Friend," as he addressed her in letters—his "best, dearest, worthiest, wisest friend in the world"—while to her he was "the tenderest of husbands," his affections "unabated," her "good man."

After her death due to typhoid, the obituary notice in Boston's *Columbian Centinel* emphasized her importance to her husband's career in public service and thus to the nation.

Possessing at every period of life the unlimited confidence, as well as affection of her husband, Abigail was admitted at all times to share largely of his thought. While, on the one hand, the activity of her mind and thorough knowledge of all branches of domestic economy enabled her almost wholly to relieve him from the cares regarding the concerns of private life; on the other, she was a friend in whom he delighted to consult in every perplexity of public affairs; and one whose counsels never failed to partake of that happy harmony which prevailed in her character. In the storm, as well as the smooth sea of life, her virtues were ever the object of his trust and veneration.

That he had been blessed in a partnership with one of the most exceptional women of her time, Adams never doubted. Her letters, he was sure, would be read for generations to come. He wrote to his granddaughter, Caroline, "Never 'by word or look' had she [Abigail] discouraged him from 'running all hazards' for their country's liberties. Willingly, bravely, she had shared with him 'in all the dangerous consequences we had to hazard.'"

For years after her death, whenever complimented about his son John Quincy and his role in national life and the part he had played as gatherer, Adams is credited as saying with emphasis, "My son had a mother!"[12]

Portrait

Chapter 7

PONDERING TWO PORTRAITS

"I DID A LOT OF damage . . . I stepped outside boundaries I had always honored and I let things happen that ordinarily I would avoid. I joined someone in compromise—in an unwise venture to fill empty spaces in our respective lives.

"That relationship grew faster and stronger than I ever anticipated, and before long I was overwhelmed. It began at a time I was harboring unmined bitterness and was afraid or unwilling to do the right thing. Seemingly overnight, it became a paralyzing emotional entanglement.

"Suddenly, I was mocking my marriage . . . I brought pain to all those around me and myself. Two years later, that renovation goes on. The apologies continue. The aftershocks are fewer but will resonate for some time."

Do these opening words represent a fictional confessional? Hardly. This regretful account gushes from the heart of a grieving, wounded, gifted, professional Christian. If you respond with sobriety—*But by the grace of God, there go I*—join with me in considering the vulnerable state of our marriages.

Assault on marriages among Christians is rampant, and leaders occupy a special high-risk category. With the discovery of each indiscretion, a relentless series of questions emerge: *How could this have happened? What went wrong? Could it have been prevented? Is there hope in the face of such distrust?*

To answer these complicated questions, I suggest we ponder two different portraits. A portrait is a picture, a profile, or an image for

101

study. Keep the testimony from the opening paragraph in your mind as we move forward with our discussion.

Portrait of Pain

Imbedded in the previous outpouring of heartache, words of warning leap off the page—words for humble consideration as we seek guidance through our own treacherous minefield of marriage.

Boundaries . . . compromise . . . empty spaces . . . bitterness . . . paralyzing emotional entanglement . . . mocking. Add to this, denial . . . indifference . . . distance.

Notice how each word begins as a whisper. Then, the decibels increase to a crescendo of concern, shouting an alarm and sending out an *all points bulletin* that life is not as it should be.

A colleague tells of driving with an annoying red light flashing from the dashboard of his automobile. His self-imposed remedy came by simply placing a thumb over the nagging signal and continuing stubbornly along his journey. Obviously, his was not a prudent decision, but pragmatism overruled. A burned out engine the next day caused him to sorely regret his tragic mistake. A vehicle is one thing; a life is another.

Are we placing our thumbs over a red light flashing on the dashboard of our marriages? A penetrating personal inventory is healthy.

I ask you, please, to pause a moment in our discussion and ask yourself:

Are my boundaries fixed where they must be to protect the oneness of my relationship with my husband?

Do I tolerate compromise for the sake of convenience?

Who or what is filling the empty spaces which are cropping up in our marriage?

Am I giving bitterness a place to grow in the garden of my heart?

Has an emotional entanglement that refuses to be brought to the light paralyzed me?

Is mocking a part of my self-talk regarding my husband and our oneness?

Am I in denial and thus less than honest in any of my above answers?

Do I accept indifference as a cheap substitute for intimacy? Has distance become my mechanism for coping in the face of disappointment and broken dreams in my marriage?

Please, if these diagnostic questions between you and the Lord raise red flags, I urge you to pray. Then, take the next step and ask for help. Pick up your phone and dial the number of a wise, godly female confidante. This person should be someone you trust implicitly, and someone mature in managing confidentiality. Ask for her guidance and ask for her to hold you accountable in moving forward.

In so doing, you will wisely bring to the light the urgency of any situation the Holy Spirit reveals. Take action, and refuse to become prey by letting the demons of darkness deceive you into believing you should continue in isolation and secrecy.

Remember, none of us is immune to the ploys of the enemy. Vigilant discernment must accompany our habits.

At this juncture, let us give attention to a second portrait.

Portrait of Protection

"Karen, do you offer any advice?" My close friend and I ached with the painful shock waves of yet another tragic story. The names were different, but the scenario sounded the same. A prominent person in ministry, a marital affair, a revelation of sordid details, all resulted in broken hearts and shattered lives.

I respect Karen tremendously and probed further for her wisdom. With a desperate sincerity I asked, "What do you think?" Her response speaks volumes:

"I have learned and continue to learn new things. The fundamental truths that have held me and guided me are nothing new. The people you and I know who are caught in these tragedies taught and believed these same truths. Self-interest became the derailer.

"When I think about the fragility of married life, I guess I would say this, 'Marriage is supported by the zillions of tiny choices we make every day. My favorite choice is to exchange my thoughts for His and my interests for His.'"

Her valuable insight serves us well. Consider her comments further.

Self Interest . . .

Tiny choices . . .

Every day . . .

Exchange my thoughts for His thoughts . . .

Exchange my interests for His interests . . .

Karen's wisdom reinforces my own conviction: This is warfare. Protection, as she suggests, will require a fight. You and I must become warriors for oneness by *guarding our hearts* and *gearing up our minds*.

Guard Your Heart!

What happens in your heart stays in your heart. Wrong! Solomon warns in Proverbs 4:23, "Above all else, guard your heart, for everything you do flows from it."

The heart is command central, and the heart houses the real, authentic you. What goes on inside a heart determines the outcome of a life. Within these confines, we make those zillion tiny choices that determine the course of our marriage.

A divided heart is dangerous. Without authenticity, inconsistency runs rampant. Living one person within and pretending to be another without depicts spiritual schizophrenia. Yet this dichotomy occurs in Christian marriages, and the lethal outcome devastates.

Granting Jesus access to our heart as Chief War Officer allows Him to build a garrison and guard our precious marital oneness.

As you and I become self-appointed heart specialists, we earnestly monitor the condition of our hearts, not just physically, but also spiritually. We check our pulse and ask, *What makes my pulse race faster, the things of God within my marriage or the things of the flesh outside of marriage?*

Next in this strategic warfare,

Gear Up Your Mind!

Refuse to be naive. John Adams said, "Facts are stubborn things; and whatever may be our wishes, our inclinations, or the dictates of our passion, they cannot alter the state of facts and evidence."

Believe a battle rages for your marriage, and determine, with God's help to engage as a warrior for the content inside your head. Scripture teaches, "Therefore, prepare your minds for action" (1 Peter 1:13, NASB).

God's arsenal is His Word, and the Holy Spirit serves as Commanding Officer. Preparation for action involves arming ourselves with the Word of God to be used by the Spirit of God to give us the abundant life of God.

The heart and mind work in tandem. Do you see the connection? What you decide in your heart gets worked out in your head and becomes lived out in your life.

We stand on safe soil when we immerse ourselves in the words of Philippians 4:8a, "Summing it all up, friends, I'd say you'll do best by filling your minds and meditating on things true, noble, reputable, authentic, compelling, gracious—the best, not the worst; the beautiful, not the ugly; things to praise, not things to curse" (MSG).

Let us ask ourselves:

What do I think about?

Where do my daydreams take me?

What fills those tiny mental gaps inside my head?

What is my behavior in the quiet of the evening?

What am I reading?

What am I watching?

Is my mental menu wholesome? Is it life-giving?

Ongoing dialogue with Jesus assists us in maintaining vigilant alertness in guarding our minds. Oneness in marriage warrants such arduous protection.

An illustration bears mentioning.

Plitviče Lakes National Park merits a place on the UNESCO World Heritage List. This world-renowned, gorgeous nature reserve rests in the mountainous region of central Croatia. Sixteen terraced lakes and cascading waterfalls offer dramatic, raw beauty for the visitor.

As trout swim in the crystal-clear streams, the water color changes constantly, depending on the daily quantity of minerals in the water and on the varying angle of sunlight. Shades shift from azure to green, then to gray or blue.

Upon discovering this spectacular gem of creation, our family savored every opportunity to hike in this unusual, raw beauty.

But there is more.

Tragically, a footnote accompanies the grandeur of this magnificent nature reserve. Warning signs appear throughout, cautioning visitors of the certain danger of stepping off the wooden walkway.

Deadly land mines—left over from Balkan Wars of the 1990s—sit menacingly undetected, waiting to explode and maim or kill any who ignore the warning. However, by staying within the confines of the clearly defined pathway, freedom prevails to soak in the surrounding beauty.

Do you see the poignant lesson?

God provides us well-marked paths to protect our hearts and minds from destruction. Freedom within the confines of boundaries allows us to relish, preserve, and protect the joy of oneness in a supernatural marriage relationship. This jewel is too precious to squander by carelessly, flippantly ignoring the consequences of stepping off into what He marked *forbidden*.

Join me in a renewed commitment to guard our hearts and fortify—gear up—our minds in protecting this glorious portrait of marriage.

Living with Eternal Intentionality™

"The thief does not come except to steal, and to kill, and to destroy. I have come that they may have life, and that they may have it more abundantly" (John 10:10, NKJV).

What (or who) currently threatens the oneness of your relationship with your husband?

How would you answer the previously posed question: *What makes my pulse race faster: the things of God within my marriage or the things of the flesh outside of my marriage?*

In the context of marriage, what are the three wisest steps you are taking to ensure authenticity and prevent the danger of a divided heart?

How are you using the Word of God in guarding your mind to fight for marital oneness?

Cameo

Mary Müller

1797–1870

In *George Müller: Delighted In God*, author Roger Steer gives insight into this remarkable marriage and ministry partnership of Mary and George. The following glimpse into Mary's life is gleaned from his work.

"Our happiness in God, and in each other, was indescribable. We had not *some* happy days every year, not a month of happiness every year; but we had twelve months of happiness in the year, and thus year after year. Often and often did I say, 'My darling, do you think there is a couple in Bristol, or in the world, happier than we are?'"

These words were spoken from the heart of George Müller, a man called by God to confront the abominable social ills effecting a population of children in England in the 1800s. The woman who shared his life, his faith, his love, and his Lord was Mary Groves Müller. She was his faithful wife and coworker in establishing orphanage houses in Bristol, England.

"Müller felt sure that it was better for him to be married, and prayed much about the choice of a life's partner. Miss Groves could hardly have been a more ideal answer to his prayers. She shared her brother's [Anthony] earnest devotion to her Lord, and fully supported him [her brother] in his decision to trust God for material supplies. According to Müller, she played the piano nicely and painted beautifully, and as for providing him with intellectual companionship, she had studied English grammar, geography, history, French, Latin and Hebrew—and she could teach George a thing or two about astronomy. On August 15, 1830, he [George] wrote asking her to be his wife; four days later, Mary accepted his proposal and they fell to their knees asking God to bless their marriage."

As the work with orphans grew to become five large orphanages housing thousands of children, no individual was ever asked for money. "Oh, it is good to trust in the living God, for He has said, 'I will never leave you or forsake you.' Expect great things from God, and great things you will have. There is no limit to what He is able to do."

"Mary was the ideal wife for the director of five large children's homes. "My darling," Müller often said to her, "God Himself singled you out for me, as the most suitable wife I could possibly wish to have had."

"During the years of trial from 1838-1846, when Müller sometimes had to use their own money in meeting expenses in the Homes, Mary never found fault with him, but joined him in prayer that God would send help. And when He did, as He always did, they often wept together for joy."

"In addition to a good education, Mary was an expert at every kind of needlework and of the appropriate types and qualities of material for clothes and linen. It was her responsibility to order hundreds of thousands of yards of all kinds of material. She would approve or reject the material when it was delivered. Every month she examined all the account books and checked hundreds of bills for the house matrons. She spent every day [at] Ashley Down [Children's Home], and paid special attention to sick children."

Of his marriage to Mary, Müller said:

"Every year our happiness increased more and more. I never saw my beloved wife at any time, when I met her unexpectedly anywhere in Bristol, without being delighted to do so. I never met her even in the Orphan Houses, without my heart being delighted to do so. Thousands of times I told her, 'My darling, I never saw you at any time, since you became my wife, without my being delighted to see you.' Further, day after day, if anyhow it could be done, I spent after dinner twenty minutes or half an hour with her. I spent these precious moments with my darling wife. There we sat, side by side, her hand in mine, as an habitual thing, having a few words of loving intercourse, or being silent, but most happy in the Lord, and in each other, whether we spoke or were silent . . . " And, as earlier noted, George Müller declared, "Our happiness in God, and in each other, was indescribable. We had not some happy days every year, not a month of happiness every year; but we had twelve months of happiness in the year, and thus year after year."

Müller believed that one of the greatest secrets of their marital bliss was that besides their times of private prayer, and family prayer, he and Mary frequently prayed together. "For many years my precious wife and I had immediately after family prayer in the morning, a short time for prayer together, when the most important points for prayer, with regard to the day, were brought before God. Should very heavy trials press on us, or should our need of any kind be particularly great, we prayed again after dinner . . . and this in times of extraordinary difficulties or necessities, might be repeated once or twice more in the afternoon . . . .

"Then, in the evening, during the last hour of our stay at the Orphan Houses, though her or my work was never so much, it was an habitually understood thing, that this hour was for prayer . . . .Our prayer, and supplication, and intercessions mingled with thanksgiving, lasted generally forty minutes, fifty minutes, and sometimes the whole hour. At these seasons we brought fifty or more different points, or persons, or circumstances before God."

"Mary Müller in 1870 was now seventy-two. For a year or two it had been obvious to Müller that her health was failing; she was growing thinner and tiring quickly. Müller tried unsuccessfully to persuade her to work less and eat more . . . Sadly she had worked too hard."

On February 6, 1870, she went Home to her beloved Lord Jesus, her earthly partnership with George Müller ended. Their lives together had been characterized by prayer, faith, and a mutual self-denial for the cause of Christ.[13]

Chapter 8

PAINTING TWO PORTRAITS

THE ARTIST OF MARRIAGE BECKONS us to join Him in the tedious endeavor of painting a portrait of oneness. Oneness, His antidote against vicious attacks threatening to sabotage this godly union, requires an enormous amount of time.

Portrait of Oneness: A Model

Marriage provides God's visual aid to the world of His relationship with His Bride, the Church. No wonder the model suffers ongoing assault as society attempts to damage, distort, defame, and redefine marriage.

God says, "Therefore a man shall leave his father and his mother and shall become united *and* cleave to his wife, and they shall become one flesh" (Genesis 2:24, AMPC). Marriage forms a human covenant with the living God. Yes, physical oneness is explicit in the text, and later I devote an entire chapter to my enthusiasm. However, in this chapter we study God's holistic plan for marriage, which incorporates more than just two bodies coming together.

In fact, His canvas holistically incorporates the spiritual, emotional, mental, and psychological union as well. The word *cleave* (adhere to, hold to, abide by, be loyal to, be faithful to) provides us with this insight.

C.S. Lewis wrote in *Mere Christianity*, "The Christian idea of marriage is based on Christ's words that a man and wife are to be regarded as a single organism—for that is what the words "one flesh" would be in modern English. And the Christians believe that when He said this, He was not expressing a sentiment but stating a fact—just as one is stating a fact when one says that a lock and its key are one mechanism, or that a violin and a bow are one musical instrument. The inventor of the human machine was telling us that two halves, the male and the female, were made to be combined together in pairs, not simply on the sexual level, but totally combined."[14]

Two pieces of a puzzle, when joined, reveal a composite, which could not be revealed if kept separate. In the same way, God designed our two lives to come together and display the portrait of Jesus, both a mystery and a marvel (Ephesians 5:32).

This artistic masterpiece takes time, and remains a work in progress over the course of a lifetime. Though the portrayal will never be perfect, it can still be perfectly *beautiful*. Smudges, color variations, contrasts of light all contribute to the overall richness of the treasured piece of art.

The enemy of our souls relentlessly shoots paintballs at this portrait, determined to mar the canvas of the Creator. So, how can you and I effectively participate with the Great Master to counter the ongoing assault? I believe fortification emerges within commitments.

Portrait of Commitment: A Means

Commitment to a Common Goal Greater than Ourselves

"Glorify the Lord with me; let us exalt His name together." These words from Psalm 34:3 offer a sterling marital mission statement. God never intended marriage to be an idol. Thus, sharing the highest common goal of bringing Him glory becomes the greatest fortification to the marriage relationship. When two people look not to themselves for satisfaction, but rather look up to glorify God, the supernatural mystery of oneness thrives.

Paradoxes emerge. The closer we, the husband and wife, grow to God, the closer we grow to each other. The more our weakness drives us to desperate dependence on Him, the stronger we become. The more we give ourselves away to the Lord and to each other, the more we individually discover the best of ourselves.

Commitment to Communication

Our friend and mentor Bobb Biehl, founder president of Masterplanning Group International, says, "Communication is the lifeblood of an organization."[15] This wisdom certainly applies to marriage, especially a marriage involved in leadership. Talking, connecting, chatting, listening, asking questions blends two otherwise isolated lives.

For Larry and me, communication stands as one of our highest values, and we guard the priority with viciousness. However, over the decades our approach to communication required flexibility, both in portion and in format, to accommodate the age and stage of our family. The setting has always been secondary to the commitment—the deliberate commitment—of staying focused, updated, and integrated into each other's lives.

With toddlers, we established a weekly date night out at a quiet restaurant. (A more detailed description of this will follow.) Later, with teenagers, Larry and I planned breakfasts at a local quaint German hotel when he returned from travels. Today, as empty nesters with a global leadership assignment, we savor our sacrosanct Saturdays, a revered, set-apart portion of time devoted to the two of us.

Over the years an unforeseen advantage transpired. I realized this when I once overheard Larry say, "Before I give you an answer, I want to talk to Debby about this. I want to get her input."

Did I hear him correctly? Larry's answer to the waiting executive would have to wait. The serious subject and the ramifications of their dialogue would carry sweeping results to affect many people. Promptness mattered. However, putting life on hold, my husband voluntarily inserted a component of tremendous importance in our relationship. He wanted to seek my counsel.

By doing so, he, perhaps, elevated my posture in the eyes of the other person, perhaps not. However, at the risk of misunderstanding from his colleague with the untimely postponement, Larry inserted the pause and confirmed his value for me as his advisor.

Keep in mind, my advisory role did not automatically come built into our marriage vows. We had to learn. (Sure, we consulted on calendars and conflicts, church and community, people and programs, duties and debts, bills and budgets—generalities.)

But I speak of a role far greater, far more serious, and far weightier—advisor, consultant, and confidante—customized to our relationship and to our lives.

This privileged place of position suffered many mistakes and a considerable number of frustrations. Setbacks marked the path. However, after 44 years of doing it both correctly and incorrectly, Larry and I operate in a sweet spot that I cherish.

For any wife of a world changer, I offer these suggestions:

Be available to listen — if not convenient at the moment, offer to carve out space soon.

Be trustworthy — make sure you have his best interest in mind.

Be committed to keeping his confidence!

Be informed — giving counsel to global leaders must take into account global events.

Be patient — expertise will come with experience; this takes time to develop.

Do not be afraid to request time to reflect before responding to his need for input.

Be realistic.

Be appreciative — let him know you value being his advisor.

Be prayerful, ever prayerful.

Though your husband will always have other advisors, your input for him will be unique. Seek to excel in this coveted opportunity. I believe the endeavor will serve to enhance your partnership.

Let me pause here and share a small treasure, our communication covenant. A proven asset in our marriage, I offer these life-giving statements for you to consider using in life with your leader.

Trust me; I will not belittle you to our children.

Trust me; I will not talk about you in a negative way to my friends.

Trust me; I will not embarrass you in public.

Furthermore, I acquired another invaluable communication resource through the advice of a wise young man. He once urged me, "Debby, when you are talking to wives married to men in leadership, be sure to tell them this: '*Do not defend your husband in public; you only belittle him. Do not correct your husband in public; you only belittle yourself.*'"

His advice later guided me through a painful communication debacle. Allow me to share personally from a painful night long ago.

I entered the building and climbed the stairs, questioning my attendance. For this town hall meeting, my husband wore a target on his back. (As a leader's wife, if you recall finding yourself in such a situation, you relate to my challenge).

Throughout the event, the audience remained emotional, hostile, antagonistic, and belligerent. Though time would come to prove the audience largely wrong, that future fact offered no solace to my heart this particular cold, winter's evening.

From my seat in the back row, I struggled to control my emotions as I vacillated between anger and tears. One moment I wanted to shout in Larry's defense; another moment I wanted to march out in protest. But within, I heard the young man's voice in my head, and I remained silent: *Do not defend your husband in public; you only belittle him. Do not correct your husband in public; you only belittle yourself.*

In utter amazement, I watched my husband raise the bar of character before that audience. And he excelled completely without my help.

Later, back at home in the comfort of our bedroom, Larry thanked me for refusing to act as Joan of Arc in his defense. When I questioned how he possibly managed to endure the undeserved humiliation, he humbly reminded me of a communication lesson learned from his hero and mentor, Bill Bright:

Larry, years ago I had to make a decision. I had to decide if I wanted to defend myself or if I wanted the Lord Jesus Christ to be my Defender. Larry, you can't have both. You must decide.

Larry charted his course through rough waters based on this wisdom, and the outcome served him well. The Lord Jesus Christ defended my husband in a manner far superior to any defense I could have mustered.

This young man and his advice remain precious to me today, for the young man is my son-in-law, Matt. Thank you, Matt. Thank you, Bill Bright.

Now, let us turn to the discussion of date night, as I mentioned earlier in the chapter. This hallowed habit of communication for Larry and me rises out of the rubble of failures to become a lighthouse of success.

Remember with me . . .

"Don't look back; whatever you do, don't look back," I kept repeating under my breath. Excitement and urgency propelled me out the heavy wooden door of our Warsaw home. I didn't want anything to block my leaving. I practically ran down the 12 concrete steps to our front gate.

Ignoring the oversized buttons, I grasped my thick wool coat around me. Winter boots, gloves, scarf, and hat were still needed in the chilly night that mocked the season of spring.

In front of me: only the spiked fence stood between my vehicle and me.

Behind me: the babysitter locked the three heavy bolts that would protect our home and its occupants for the next three hours.

This was Friday date night, and my husband and I were going on a date! Larry would travel by taxi from his clandestine office, and I would drive our car to join him. The destination was a small restaurant at the U.S. Embassy open to any American citizen.

Routinely, for years, Larry and I met weekly at the American Club in Warsaw. No membership was required, just a U.S. passport. This tiny, modest venue provided the one place in the entire country where we could order a bacon cheeseburger, a Dr. Pepper, and a piece of cheesecake.

We relished this reprieve in our complicated, covert lives. Sitting in our standard booth, with our standard menu, we talked, sipped Dr. Pepper, and connected. Though we guarded our conversation for security reasons, this environment gave us time to talk and a place to talk.

Long before Warsaw, Larry and I established a date night routine. Early in our marriage, we made a commitment to preserve this once-a-week tradition. Doggedly, we worked to protect our sacred appointment.

It was never easy, no.

Different seasons brought different challenges. With babies, we just wanted sleep, not conversation. With toddlers, there was the hassle of arranging a babysitter. Having school-age children brought the hurdle of homework. And with teenagers, their activities filled our calendars to capacity, leaving little margin for time alone.

One would think the empty nest allowed time, time, and more time for date night. Not so! Larry and Debby became full-fledged workaholics. Making the mistake of working way beyond normal hours, date night vanished. We rationalized that since we were together nearly 24/7, date night was unnecessary.

Bad idea. Our communication and our marriage suffered, and we wisely called a halt to the foolish patterns challenging our agreement.

You ask, "Is this really worth the bother?" I understand your question, and I answer that I believe it is. Looking back over more than four decades of marriage, I avow the significance.

A date night:

- punctuates our busy lives with a pause, a much-needed relational pause
- protects from the damaging distance that threatens to creep into a marriage; herein, we make a concerted effort to engage rather than to simply exist in our relationship
- provides an opportunity to laugh, to listen, to connect, and to remember why we chose each other
- points forward to a future of life and dreams together. Like crossing a fast flowing, turbulent stream, on date nights we reach out and help each jump from one slippery stone to another

Simple ground rules encourage success. Here are my suggestions:

- Declare testy topics off-limits: finances, problems at work, Christmas with which set of parents. (Not here, not now; another time, another place.)
- Determine to persevere even when your best efforts derail.
- Don't be deterred by too busy, too tired, too complicated, or too expensive.
- Decide before you leave home to be a blessing to your husband. Then, ask God, in the power of the Holy Spirit, to bring this to pass.

Forty-four years and counting, I repeat, we got this one right.

Are you still with me? Let us march ahead now and consider the all-time eternal game changer, forgiveness, and its role in godly communication.

Commitment to Forgiveness

Again from Bill Bright, Larry and I learned the four greatest statements in marriage: *I am sorry. I was wrong. I love you. Will you forgive me?*

Ruth Graham said it this way: *A happy marriage is the union of two good forgivers.*[16]

Equally as poignant, is this statement from our pastor, Ronnie Stevens: *Forgiveness never goes to a deserving person.*

In a vibrant marriage growing in oneness, forgiveness operates as a way of life. A holy healing takes place when we forgive, so I urge you to keep short accounts; be a partner who is quick to forgive. In fact, forgiveness protects against a poisonous root of bitterness warned against in Hebrews 12:15: "See to it that no one falls short of the grace of God and that no bitter root grows up to cause trouble and defile many."

Early in our marriage, Larry and I implemented a principle: We refused to go to sleep with unresolved conflict. Granted, some long nights occurred, but the priceless results proved the practice worthwhile.

Later, unsuspectingly, we learned the ramifications of this commitment. At the celebration of our 25th wedding anniversary hosted by our children, these words were shared: *I have taken great comfort in knowing you are so committed to each other that you would not sleep until your conflicts are resolved.*

This comment verifies that forgiveness and the keeping of short accounts bear long, lasting dividends.

Now, my reader friend, we move to our final communication commitment.

Commitment to Confront the Enemy of Oneness

Living parallel lives stands out as one of the greatest deterrents to relational oneness. As a vogue model in today's culture, this chic arrangement offers us freedom and autonomy, but robs us of intimacy. Follow the progression as it begins with distraction.

Distraction says that consuming focus elsewhere is more important than focus on each other and the development of our marriage relationship.

Distraction leads to distance. Distance depicts parallel lives, meaning our lives run on separate tracks, and our tracks seldom overlap.

Distance leads to discouragement. Discouragement settles like a dark storm cloud over our relationship, and discouragement makes it harder to persevere and easier to pull away.

Discouragement leads to disillusionment. Disillusionment speaks lies and tempts husband and wife to conclude that marriage is too hard, the assistant is too pretty, the children's soccer coach is too fit, you are too busy, and I am too bored.

Then, disillusionment leads to . . . well; let's not go there!

Simply living under the same roof, sharing the same address, sharing the same bed does not insulate us from living on tracks of parallel lives. However, communication—along with bulldog tenacity in the power of the Holy Spirit—guards against our lives drifting into aloneness and serves to guide our lives into a God-inspired oneness.

Building oneness—emotional, mental, physical, psychological intimacy—will always prove hard and challenging. However, as you and I labor over a canvas, working with the Master Artist, we are creating a beautiful masterpiece, not a quick snapshot, for our portrait of marriage.

Living with Eternal Intentionality™

"May the God who gives endurance and encouragement give you the same attitude of mind toward each other that Christ Jesus had, so that with one mind and one voice you may glorify the God and Father of our Lord Jesus Christ" (Romans 15:5-6).

What is your opinion of C.S. Lewis' quote from *Mere Christianity*?

Describe what life would look like for you and your husband to adopt Psalm 34:3 as your marriage's mission statement?

Do you have a communication covenant between the two of you? If not, what are your thoughts on adopting the one suggested in this chapter?

Think back on an occasion when you participated as an advisor for your husband. What did you learn?

Can you recall a situation when you attempted to be your husband's defender? Was the outcome positive or negative?

Where in your marriage is a pattern of forgiveness most needed?

Before we talk about the S word, allow me to acquaint you with a woman who was a champion in building a marriage of oneness with her leader husband. Meet Barbara Spooner.

Cameo

Barbara Spooner

1771-1847

"Barbara Spooner, who became the wife of William Wilberforce, was a remarkable lady. Two weeks after their initial meeting, Wilberforce proposed marriage, to which Barbara agreed. They were married a month later, six weeks after they met. The marriage of William and Barbara was so strong, so unshakable that historians agree it had an impact on the institution of marriage in England for the next 50 years. They were held as such an example of strength and fidelity that those around them—and around the country—took notice. The pair ran against the culture of the time, which said it was acceptable to demean women or to be unfaithful to your wife. Add to that Barbara's constant exposure to the public—she was very much a public figure in her husband's life. All these things combined so well that their marriage—and the strength of it—became public knowledge. They raised the bar and modeled something for their culture that was rarely seen at the time. More importantly, Barbara had a tremendous impact on her husband. She was his constant encourager, his staunch ally, and his fiercest friend. She helped him carry the abolition banner for the rest of his life."[17]

Chapter 9

NO NEED FOR BATHSHEBA

A SCENE IN THE MOVIE *Walk the Line* captivates me. The venue is the recording studio in Memphis, Tennessee. The Tennessee Trio just finished singing what they deemed their best, and yet the exasperated, bored record producer Sam Phillips owner asked (paraphrase), "Mr. Cash, is this the best you've got in you? If you had just been hit by a truck, you were out there in that gutter dying, and you were given the chance to sing just one more song, what would that song be?"[18]

What occurred next would rock the world of music. With inhibition cast aside and the *boom-chicka-boom* background rolling, Johnny Cash reached deep within himself, and in that distinctive, bass-baritone voice found the passion to sing and patent a style that still brings a smile to country music lovers worldwide.

Though not a musician, I ask myself the same question, "If I had just one chapter left in me to write, what would that chapter be?" *Boom-chicka-boom*, this chapter on *sex*. With inhibition cast aside, I reach deep within and share with passion my passion for this passionate subject.

Following my speaking to a large audience where I referenced my conviction on "no need for Bathsheba," our Cru® president Steve Douglass said, "Debby, I think you should write on this. I've already heard from several individuals who agree."

I, the wife of a leader, believe in the power of sex in the life of a leadership couple. I am not a doctor, a counselor, a psychiatrist, or a therapist. I am just Debby. Within theses pages I write to encourage you—no, to urge you to enjoy all God planned for you when you are in bed with your husband. The sexual relationship is important for any wife, but paramount for those of us who live with world changers. Without parroting what I have heard or what I have read, I simply share what I believe.

Allow me to share a deeply personal illustration.

As this particular day dawned, a jolt struck at the core of my being. I realized that I shared our marriage with a mistress. I never dreamed this would happen. The lightning bolt of realization instantly shattered my heart into a thousand smithereens. I felt betrayed and deceived. This mistress had a name. Her name was *Travel*.

With the explosion of unprecedented ministry opportunities, I watched the activity around me escalate. The intensity of the pace of city campaigns, conferences, and Christ-centered chaos made me feel like I was losing my husband. Our lives—and our relationship—seemed to be slipping through my grasp. He seemed to either be going out on a trip or coming back in from a trip.

In quiet desperation, I took my overwhelming frustration to the Lord, and He took me to His Word. What God tenderly taught me changed the course of my attitude and actions.

Read with me in 2 Samuel 11:1-4:

> In the spring, at the time when kings go off to war, David sent Joab out with the king's men and the whole Israelite army. They destroyed the Ammonites and besieged Rabbah. But David remained in Jerusalem.
>
> One evening David got up from his bed and walked around on the roof of the palace. From the roof he saw a woman bathing. The woman was very beautiful,and David sent someone to find out about her. The man said, "She is Bathsheba,the daughter of Eliam and the wife of Uriah the Hittite." Then David sent messengers to get her. She came to him, and he slept with her.

"In the spring, at the time when kings go off to war . . . David remained in Jerusalem."

Please do not miss the profundity.

In the spring of the year . . .

kings (David was a king) . . .

go off to war.

Keep reading.

David. Was. In. Jerusalem.

David did not go off to fight according to his God-given kingly duty. Rather than appropriately leading his troops in battle, he remained behind in Jerusalem. One evening as he walked around on the roof of the palace, he saw a beautiful woman bathing, inquired about her, learned she was Bathsheba, then sent for her, and slept with her. Staying behind in Jerusalem, led him into trouble. Had he been on the battlefield—in the center of God's will—how different the scenario might have been. His adultery with Bathsheba resulted from not leaving Jerusalem and leading his army as God created him to lead.

Shockingly, upon reading this account, the Holy Spirit opened my eyes, and I prayed, "Oh, Lord, forgive me. I get it. I want my husband to be in the center of Your will. When You want him to be away fighting in the battle, I want to support his being present there, right in the center of Your will. I do not want to stand in the way, and I do not want to block his contribution to Your cause. With blessing, I choose to release him to go. I will be here when he returns home. There will be no need for Bathsheba. By Your grace, in our marriage, there will be no need for Bathsheba."

May I gently ask, "Is there a mistress in your marriage?" The mistress in our marriage bore the name *Travel.* What about yours? Is it your church, or the pressure of the weekly Sunday sermon? Is it your elder board? Maybe it is weariness, boredom, or busyness? It could be discouragement, distractions, or disillusionment. Whether it's toddlers, teenagers, motherhood, or menopause, I encourage you to turn with me to the Bible. Perhaps a surprising, fresh awareness awaits us.

Sex is Supremely Spiritual

Dallas Willard in the *Divine Conspiracy* writes for us, "The intent in marriage is a union of two people that is even deeper than the union of parents and children or any other human relationship. They are to become 'one flesh,' one natural unit, building one life, which therefore could never lose or substitute for one member and remain a whole life (Matthew 19:5; Genesis 2:24)."[19]

In His love for us, God the Father designed a safe place for pure pleasure in our human existence. Furthermore, He is honored when we enjoy His sacred provision. The sexual relationship is a gift that was created for pleasure before it was created for procreation. This extraordinary phenomenon is for our good and for His glory.

Genesis 2:25 states, "Adam and his wife were both naked, and they felt no shame." "Felt no shame" means they were not disappointed; they were satisfied. This perfect plan was in a perfect place and they had perfect bodies. To me it sounds like a perennial honeymoon.

"Every good and perfect gift is from above, coming down from the Father" (James 1:17a)—including sex. God has given us such a marvelous gift.

Granted, we are sickened when we consider the world's cheapening of what God made holy. But, do we fully value what God has placed in our hands? Do we honor, appreciate, and invest in this rare and beautiful treasure? Or rather, do we as Christians toss it back to God and say, "I'm tired of this; I'm bored. I don't like it. You can have it back. Have you got anything else for me, God?" This sounds silly, but I wonder if, perhaps, our actions tend to border on the pharisaical.

Imagine opening a lovely package and discovering an exquisite Herend porcelain vase. Fascination, appreciation, and admiration overwhelm us. What would happen, however, if over time, enthusiasm for the once-cherished gift wanes, and disinterest descends?

Careless treatment and causal neglect ensue. The beautiful vase becomes just *a headache*. It takes too much time to maintain, and other more dazzling objects vie for attention. Without regard for its value, we yawn, dismissively shove the treasure in a closet, close the door, and walk away.

As pedestrian as the illustration sounds, perhaps insight rests within the simplicity. Let us continue.

God the Son died on the cross to provide an intimacy for us that sin sought to destroy. His death, burial, and resurrection give a glorious quality to sex that we never, otherwise, would know. Enmity and strife in human relationships on every level undergo transformation under His Lordship. This is most assuredly applicable to sexual intimacy between a husband and wife.

Thankfully, He did not leave us stranded without instruction. In consistency with His character, God has provided guidance. In fact, The Bible is a marvelous manual on sex. Ponder Proverbs 5:18b-19: "Take pleasure in the wife of your youth. Let her breasts always satisfy you; be lost in her love forever (HCSB)."

Furthermore, God the Holy Spirit stands as the best sex therapist. John 16:13a says, "But when he, the Spirit of truth, comes, he will guide you into all the truth." I take this promise literally. He wants to guide us into the truth regarding any problems, tensions, strains, and frustrations in our sexual lives.

What if we allowed a fresh, holy awe to descend upon the physical aspect of our marital relationship? Contemplate anew the impact of completely enjoying God's beautiful gift of our sexual relationship.

Sex is Supremely Important

If you want to make a difference in your husband's life, make a difference in his bed. Even if *romance* isn't his thing, I can assure you that sex is.

Why is this physical union so important? God knew a married couple needed this haven of happy holiness. In fact, He has instructed us not to deprive each other from enjoying the pleasure of sex except by mutual agreement for a time of prayer (1 Corinthians 7:5).

Herein we acknowledge the world, the flesh, and the devil are no respecters of persons. The fact that your husband is a leader only makes him more prey. The thief wants to steal, kill and destroy what God wants to bless (John 10:10).

Our culture is inundated with information, and yet we are starved for intimacy. Today the industry of sex is shockingly convenient. The internet and its provision of easily-accessible pornography plows inroads into marriages where angels fear to tread. Thus, I make no apology for my persistence in speaking to the priority of pleasure in marriage.

My homespun theology regarding the priority of physical pleasure goes like this:

Sex is:

*the most **we** part of us, the epitome of oneness*

the ultimate in intimacy, a supremely personal sanctuary

a shelter in the hurricanes of life, offering us a haven in the storms

a gated-community for just the two of us

a Teflon for trials; a celebration for commemorations

a sleeping pill, better than any prescribed medication

a pain pill, soothing against disappointments and heartaches

always available, always a gift

like a classic, it has stood the test of time; like a wine, it grows better with age like an antique, but not antiquated

flexible, versatile, comforting, energizing

a companion between husband and wife through all seasons of life

a guard from moral temptation

comes with God's Good Housekeeping seal of approval, a lifetime warranty,

the gift that keeps on giving

for both husband and wife, for richer or poorer

priority, protection and pleasure.

"Therefore what God has joined together, let no man put asunder!" (Matthew 19:6, MEV, exclamation mine).

Dr. Pepper Schwartz is a Professor of Sociology at the University of Washington in Seattle. She is the author or co-author of numerous books, magazine articles, and website columns, and is a television personality on the subject of sexuality. She holds liberal views, but her content on NPR's *On Point* news program titled, "The Way of the Affair: the Science and Psychology of Infidelity" is remarkable. When asked her advice for couples wanting to avoid infidelity, her comments to listeners bear thoughtful consideration.

Just never put it on automatic pilot

Be sexually, emotionally engaged

Have dates

Be lovers; do not turn into parents who are an efficient work unit

Make sure that romance and that connection and that intimacy never goes away. "It's the best insurance I can think of."[20]

Thank you, Dr. Schwartz.

Yes, sex is supremely important for husbands, for wives, and for the glory of God.

Sex is Supremely Personal

Sex, as stated prior, is the most *we* component of us; it is also the most personal part of our person. We do not have license to sin outside of marriage, but we definitely receive God's blessing to be creative within.

What is forbidden beyond the borders finds freedom within the hedges of home. Here a husband and wife's incompleteness finds a mysterious completeness on a spiritual, physical, and emotional level. The only requirement in this epitome of personal pursuit is confidentiality. Sizzling or soothing, sex meanders like a river through the course of marriage.

Think about this: Music, throughout the ages, has been known as the language of the heart. Thus, our sexual relationship is like a sheet of music where the two of us write our own lifetime symphony.

Tempo, mood, and volume are ours for creativity and personal expression. *Allegro,* lively and fast; *andante,* medium speed; *presto,* very fast; or *adagio,* slow movement, restful, and at ease. These tempos each bestow their unique contribution.

Moods vacillate between highs and lows—major, when life seems positive, affirming, and minor, for those seasons defined as mysterious, and melancholic. However, continuity will be preserved through intermezzo, the short movements or interludes that connect the main parts of the composition.

Whether it's the minuet, that slow and graceful dance, or a musette (a Baroque dance with a drone-bass), let us dance and make music with the one whom God has given us to love and cherish.

Resist monotone; incorporate modulation and transposition to another key when life pushes in that direction. Even compose your own sexual sonata, the music with four movements. As each sonata differs in tempo, rhythm, and melody, the overall holds together by subject and style.

Yes, within the covenant of marriage, God gives us the freedom to customize our lovemaking. I encourage you to allow hushed habits to travel with you through the changing phases of life and inevitable stages of family development.

Furthermore, snacks and appetizers are not just for a culinary menu, and pit stop is not a term limited to a petrol station. Even a quickie before work can make a world of difference before heading into a hectic schedule. Though banquets sometimes have to wait, closeness can continue.

Prioritize your oneness by asking, "Why not now?" Even former President George W. Bush's father-in-law, at George and Laura's rehearsal dinner, put forth this advice: "If you go home for lunch, make sure you wear the same tie when you return to the office"[21]

To intentionally embrace this personal pursuit, you must be willing to dismantle the myths. What do I mean by myths? The following:

Sex is for men. Read the Song of Solomon.

Making love is only for the bedroom. Consider from sea to shining sea; boats and trains; hospitals and hotels.

I am only to respond. Try initiating and watch what happens.

Sex is just for nighttime. There is a reason why there are 24 hours in one day.

I have to be perfect to have good sex. Not true; just get in bed.

We are too old. Are you older than Abraham and Sarah?

I'm too fat. Weight never inhibits an orgasm.

Think on this: You are the only one whom God has granted the privilege to provide pleasure to this man. One of the greatest ways to ensure that he enjoys intercourse is for you to enjoy intercourse as well. And truthfully, I believe you just might enjoy it more than he does.

Sex is So Much Fun

What does it take to have a sanctified, sizzling, sex life from newlywed newness through the empty-nest nostalgia? I offer five words of suggestion: consistency, attitude, prayer, conversation, and celebration.

Consistency

If communication is the lifeblood of a marriage, then consistency is the key to a vibrant sexual relationship. Granted, appetites will vary with a gentle ebb and flow as thermostats shift up and down, and as illnesses and surgeries require attention.

But I encourage you, don't give up. Refuse to yield to deceit, disappointment, or distractions of work and of the world. With care and attention, "the fireworks of youth" can give way to "the holy heat" of embers that have been well tended over the course of a lifetime. If from time to time you need to install updates, don't hesitate. Maybe your software needs to be upgraded to include a pair of leopard-print thongs. Perhaps his update needs to incorporate Viagra (or its more cost-friendly generic). I don't know. Yet I do know that consistency is invaluable.

Attitude

Attitude and appetite go hand in hand. My recommendation is to get your mind in gear and focus. A major secret to success is mental engagement. You might purchase all the right equipment: candles, lotions, and lingerie. Yet, these are nullified if your head is elsewhere.

As well, stay light hearted, and accept the occasional disappointment. Resist the temptation to take yourself too seriously. Performance and perfection are poison in any area of life, but particularly destructive in the bed.

Prayer

That's right, prayer. Ask God to give a holy desire for what He has already blessed. Ask Him for an increased thirst and appetite for what He has already provided.

Conversation

Assumptions are lethal. Never think your husband knows what you like, and never think you know what pleases him. Verbalize what is on your mind. Discuss your preferences, voice your dislikes, and affirm your delights.

Celebration

Relax and enjoy the rewards of your faithfulness to each other. Embrace the euphoria of God's gift with God's blessing.

In closing, let me say that you and I have talked about the naked truth and the not-so-naughty bare facts. My prayer, dear reader, is that you will continue to ask God to enlarge the creative borders of your lovemaking with your beloved for as long as you both shall live—for His glory and for your good.

Living with Eternal Intentionality™

"God blessed them . . . " (Genesis 1:28).

Is there a mistress in your marriage? If so, what is her name?

If left totally up to you and God, how would you orchestrate the sex life you have always wanted?

God created a safe place for pure pleasure in our human existence. What incremental steps do you want to pursue to fully enjoy His good gift to you (James 1:17)?

Please articulate an item from your own homespun theology.

What lesson from Dr. Schwartz do you see as a relevant conversation topic between you and your husband?

After reading this chapter, have you become aware of a myth needing to be dismissed? If so, what is the myth?

In what way do you see prayer as the go-to solution in pursuing sexual oneness with your husband?

Cameo

Winona Watts

1902-1998

I HEARD HER VOICE.

I heard her voice a few days before our big event. When I drove up to her lovely, white-brick home that hot, humid, June afternoon, I spotted her working among the flowers in her yard. There she was, weeding and cutting daylilies to share with a neighbor.

This beloved woman felt like an extra grandmother to me. In my growing up years, she played a significant role. So much more than just a neighbor, her eye contact and focused attention always made me feel loved and valued. Her work ethic and variety of hobbies and skills made her every bit as resourceful as a Google search engine.

I closed the door of my car, and she looked up. Always kind and friendly, she stopped her work for a moment of conversation. Since neither one of us had long to visit, we just stood outdoors in the heat as we chatted.

Like always, she took time to express a genuine interest in my life, my ministry, and my future. This day's conversation focused on my upcoming wedding—the plans, the parties, the persistent to-do list. And, yes of course, the flowers. Talking to her made me smile. I sensed she truly shared my excitement and my enthusiasm as a soon-to-be bride.

Suddenly—almost abruptly—she stopped our conversation. Brushing the hair off her forehead, and with a wistful look in her eyes, she traveled back in time. Now a widow, she seemed to revisit a part of her life I never knew—a life, which long ago had come and gone.

Putting her hands on her hips, she drew closer to my face and commanded my attention. This woman, standing in her yard, spoke with a determined authority that shocks me still to this day. "Honey, let me just tell you one thing. Drop your modesty with your petticoat." Lest I missed the meaning, she repeated her statement. "Drop your modesty with your petticoat."

I nodded and smiled. As I made my way to my car and quietly drove away, I had the sense I had just been offered a gift, advice which had stood the test of time.

I heard her voice again the predawn morning of our special day. My eyes opened and I felt a one-of-a-kind feeling: This was my wedding day! At 5 a.m., she and my mother were outside my bedroom window clipping gardenias. These blooms would lavishly decorate the church and fill the bridesmaid bouquets. The delicate blossoms needed to be cut fresh before the sun rose and damaged them.

I heard her voice again that night, our special wedding night. The long-awaited moment finally arrived, and we were incredibly alone as husband and wife.

Countless times, down through the decades, *I heard her voice* as it traveled with me to make an indelible mark on my marriage. "Honey, drop your modesty with your petticoat." Thank you Mamaw Watts.

She got it right.

Thank God I listened.

Promises

Chapter 10

PROMISES, POWERFUL PROMISES FOR YOU, THE LEADER'S WIFE

AS I BEGIN WRITING THIS chapter, I pray, *Lord, how do I tell these dear readers how wonderful You are? How You are everything they will ever need? How You will be there for every situation? How do I put on paper the passion that I have for You and Your faithfulness?*

Singing the words "Through many dangers toils and snares I have already come" always takes me to a time and place long ago. In Poland, on a frigid night in December 1981, the heat in our yellow Fiat was woefully inadequate. We shivered from the cold and watched the military tanks roll past us.

The Communist authorities declared martial law, and the entire world watched and held its breath. What would happen to the Polish people? Would there be an all-out military attack?

The Polish population feared this dreaded collision. For months, political strikes, student protests, and street riots marked the landscape of this nation seeking freedom from Communism. On December 13, the surge shifted. "Enough!" The Soviet Union issued an ultimatum to General Jaruzelski, Poland's leader: "Bring your people under submission or we will do it for you."

Now, Soviet tanks lined the Polish-Soviet border. They waited impatiently to give the Polish military one final chance with martial law, State of War, to restore order. The clock ticked like a time bomb. If the government failed, Leonid Brezhnev and the Kremlin sat poised to succeed.

An iron fist around the throat of freedom determined to cut off the very breath of this nation we vicariously called our own, and the bloody confrontation seemed imminent. What I saw is forever seared in my memory.

Tanks, column after column of Polish military in Russian-made equipment, moved into the city to crush a population who had dreamed of democracy. As I peered through the foggy glass of our vehicle, I was shocked at the force of power on display. Fear with its own cruel icy feel threatened to control me.

Then suddenly, in that cold car, in the midst of the international Cold War, deep inside enemy territory, I knew we were not alone. I heard an angel chorus, and it wasn't singing "Silent Night." The heavenly host sang the one song I needed to hear: "Through many dangers, toils and snares I have already come. 'Tis grace hath brought me safe thus far, and grace will lead me home."

Living a dual life as undercover missionaries in a Communist country during the Cold War held unusual complexities. Yet, as challenging as it was, I always considered it an indescribable privilege to be beside my husband in bringing the light of the glorious Gospel to a land of darkness.

My life alongside my Christ-committed leader stands as one of life's most honorable and blessed callings. Not for a nanosecond would I vacate the spot customized by God for me. I treasure the privilege to voice with Larry, "We Have Decided to Follow Jesus."

God's presence has permeated every single *danger, toil, and snare.* He has never failed to walk with me and abundantly provide for me in every situation that I have encountered. His faithfulness is inscribed on the tablet of my heart, and it is to that faithfulness that I want to speak.

I am confident you agree that, as a leader's wife, you and I need resources beyond our own. This exceptional calling requires exceptional assets. In Him alone we find the unfathomable capacity to embrace our pilgrimage with fullness and confidence.

His supernatural promises serve as the provision for the journey: the promise of His presence, the promise of His protection, the promise of His provision. We will consider them one by one.

Supernatural Promises

The Promise of His Presence

But now, this is what the Lord says —

He who created you, Jacob,

He who formed you, Israel:

Do not fear, for I have redeemed you;

I have summoned you by name; you are mine.

When you pass through the waters,

I will be with you;

and when you pass through the rivers,

they will not sweep over you.

When you walk through the fire,

you will not be burned;

the flames will not set you ablaze.

For I am the Lord your God,

the Holy One of Israel, your Savior (Isaiah 43:1-3a).

A key word commands our attention: *Through.*

Through . . . not around

Detours, shortcuts, and alternate routes do not exist when we desire to walk intimately with God. In our human frailness, we yearn to go around, under, over—anywhere but through. Yet, God is not in the detour, shortcuts, or alternate routes. God is in the midst. We must march right through whatever His will places in our path. Opting out is not an option, if we want to walk in intimacy with Him. He is right with us in the middle of the challenge, chaos, or crisis.

Through . . . not forever

A sliver of optimism emerges. Through is the holy *aha* assuring me I am not stuck here forever. The word *through* inherently implies there is another side to this dilemma, and hope emerges that I will make it there.

Through . . . not alone

Hard places are holy places, because He is there. He will always be present. Destruction will not dominate, and disaster will not dictate. Not ultimately. Through all the waters, rivers and fires, God says, "I will be with you." For you and me, He longs to demonstrate His loving companionship in the mucky midst of challenge, chaos, or crisis — our waters, rivers, and fires of life with a leader.

Waters, rivers, and fires constitute threatening forces of nature. They possess the potential to destroy and the power to devastate. In life, terrorizing waters, rivers, and fires come in various forms. Some are actually physical, but many are emotional, mental, even relational. Perhaps, relational is the hardest.

Life with a leader involves fallout for the leader's wife. Do you agree? I remember a challenging situation that grew in difficulty, intensity, and pain because my husband was the leader. One morning, my spirit broke under the weight of the circumstances, and in the privacy of my home office, I fell to my knees, crying out to the Lord.

"Lord, I cannot continue in this ongoing hurt and pain. You must intervene and provide deliverance for me from the suffering created by this miserable situation. You promised to be with me. You promised to provide a window of escape (1 Corinthians 10:13). Where are You, God?!"

As I ended my heart-wrenching prayer, the doorbell rang. Imagine my breathless shock as I opened the door and discovered a dear friend standing on my doorstep. Without fanfare, she stepped into my foyer with these words: "I want you to know I am concerned for your painful predicament, and I am here to pray with you." (Keep in mind—she had *no* idea of the details of my conversation with God.) I remained speechless. I felt like Rhoda when she saw Peter standing at the door in Acts 12:13-14.

In the privacy of my living room, my friend and I prayed together. As we did, an amazing miracle occurred. The menacing grip broke. I experienced God's presence with me as never before. He heard my cry for help, and He intervened supernaturally to demonstrate His comfort.

He and I continued to walk through the white-knuckled waters, yet His presence remained more real than the power of the problem or the power of the circumstances. His grace enabled me to thrive, not just survive, within that difficult season.

A brilliant lesson emerges for you and me: God does what no husband can possibly do by providing His resources of peace, strength, and joy—how firm a foundation!

How firm a foundation, ye saints of the Lord,

Is laid for your faith in His excellent Word!

What more can He say than to you He hath said,

You, who unto Jesus for refuge have fled?

In every condition, in sickness, in health;

In poverty's vale, or abounding in wealth;

At home and abroad, on the land, on the sea,

As thy days may demand, shall thy strength ever be.

Fear not, I am with thee, O be not dismayed,

For I am thy God and will still give thee aid;

I'll strengthen and help thee, and cause thee to stand

Upheld by My righteous, omnipotent hand.

When through the deep waters I call thee to go,

The rivers of woe shall not thee overflow;

For I will be with thee, thy troubles to bless,
And sanctify to thee thy deepest distress.

When through fiery trials thy pathways shall lie,
My grace, all sufficient, shall be thy supply;
The flame shall not hurt thee; I only design
Thy dross to consume, and thy gold to refine.

The soul that on Jesus has leaned for repose,
I will not, I will not desert to its foes;
That soul, though all hell should endeavor to shake,
I'll never, no never, no never forsake.

— John Keene, 1787

The Promise of His presence provides the promise of His protection, our second consideration.

The Promise of His Protection

> "As for everyone who comes to me and hears my words and puts them into practice, I will show you what they are like. They are like a man building a house, who dug down deep and laid the foundation on rock. When a flood came, the torrent struck that house but could not shake it, because it was well built" (Luke 6:47-48).

Here, I alert you to the word *When.*

When . . . not if.

In the face of a crisis, there is no time for preparation. As the wife of a leader, your life will include storms on a regular basis. Will you be prepared? Jesus' teaching in Luke 6 provides three phrases instructing us how to prepare and thus how to experience His protection.

Come to Him,

Hear His words,

and

Put them into practice.

Come to Him: We come to Him once for salvation; continue to come to Him for the constructing our lives.

Hear His Words: We hear His Words by giving ear to what He has to say to us. His Words provide the building materials needed, and He is the foundation on which we are to build.

Put them into practice: We are instructed to put His Words into practice, regularly, habitually, eagerly, and consistently.

Thus, when the floods and torrents come—and they will come—you and I will not be shaken; we will not collapse. Such a well-built foundation (spiritual, mental, emotional) remains supernaturally solid, deep, and fixed on the Rock. Stand we will.

My hope is built on nothing less
Than Jesus' blood and righteousness.
I dare not trust the sweetest frame,
But wholly trust in Jesus' Name.
On Christ the solid Rock I stand,
All other ground is sinking sand;
All other ground is sinking sand.
When darkness seems to hide His face,
I rest on His unchanging grace.
In every high and stormy gale,
My anchor holds within the veil.
His oath, His covenant, His blood,
Support me in the whelming flood.
When all around my soul gives way,
He then is all my Hope and Stay.
When He shall come with trumpet sound,
Oh may I then in Him be found.

Dressed in His righteousness alone,

Faultless to stand before the throne.

– Edward Mote, 1834

The third promise He gives us is the promise of His provision.

The Promise of His Provision

"His divine power has given us everything we need for a godly life through our knowledge of him who called us by his own glory and goodness" (2 Peter 1:3).

Everything . . . Nothing . . . Anything.

Giving us everything we need means giving us Himself. His everything—for our nothing. When we have Him, we truly have everything we need. *Everything* . . . not a few things, not some things, rather everything with a capital E.

His everything meets our nothing, and the result is everything, exactly what we need for anything that comes our way. Whether we find ourselves in green pastures or in a lion's den, we have everything we need through our knowledge of Him.

Nothing. God plus nothing is more than enough. God plus _____ (fill in the blank) is more than enough? No. God plus *nothing* is more than enough.

However, we must always answer the question, "Will I allow His everything to be enough for my anything?"

Living in one's own resources inherently blocks His power. The two are mutually exclusive. When we reach the end of ourselves, we tap into the His fullness. Not until you and I reach our own nothing can we grasp the glorious sufficiency of His everything.

He giveth more grace when the burdens grow greater,

He sendeth more strength when the labors increase,

To added affliction He addeth His mercy,

To multiplied trials, His multiplied peace.

His love has no limit, His grace has no measure,
His power no boundary known unto men,
For out of His infinite riches in Jesus,
He giveth and giveth and giveth again.
When we have exhausted our store of endurance,
When our strength has failed ere the day is half-done,
When we reach the end of our hoarded resources,
Our Father's full giving is only begun.

– Annie Flint Johnson

He has given us His very great and precious promises so that through them we may participate in the divine nature. His presence, His protection, and His provision are fully available.

However, I am confronted with a choice. As I related earlier, these supremely supernatural resources are available from God Himself. Yet, for these resources to become my own, I must make a decision. We give attention, now, to the significance of decision.

Supernatural Choice

I sat ensconced in a cocoon of solitude. As the concrete walls on two sides nearly touched my shoulders, the nook was mine—my haven.

Seclusion came at a high price with three small children in our home in Warsaw. Larry graciously fed them breakfast in this season of our lives so that I could be alone with Jesus. Morning after morning I would come to my sanctuary to meet with the Lord. The effort was worth it; He always met me.

On this dismal fall day, I gazed out the window. A thick morning fog hung heavily in the air; the trees had no leaves. Coal pollution poured from smoking chimneys. Across the street, the neighbor's house stood under construction. Indeed, a lifeless gray colored everything.

I needed these moments, and I needed the steaming, rich brown coffee served in my favorite mug.

Life felt like a runaway express train, with my husband as the conductor. At this speed, I felt vulnerable as waves of reality rolled over me.

Shoving aside challenges of a clandestine pioneering ministry, shutting out Communist propaganda, and slamming the door on the voice of the enemy of my soul, I came to my only source of strength.

Lord, I need something to lift me out of the miry clay. (I pictured a childhood situation when I walked too near a river with quicksand, and became frightfully stuck. Fortunately, strong arms came to my rescue, and lifted me up and out of danger.) *I need strong arms this morning to lift me out of life's miry clay.*

Opening my Bible to the next portion of Scripture in my ongoing plan, I read Daniel 4:34:

"I, Nebuchadnezzar, raised my eyes toward heaven, and my sanity was restored." **What? I read and reread the verse:** *"I, Nebuchadnezzar, raised my eyes toward heaven, and my sanity was restored."*

As spiritual reality slowly sank in, I nearly shouted. "That's it!" Incredulous, I devoured the words crafting this statement of high impact.

God's Message was clear. *Look at Me*—not at the nasty street, not at the crummy weather, not at your lack of sleep, not at the hostile Communist government, not at the distance from family, not at the needs of the little ones you so love, not at your husband's daunting schedule. No, *Look at Me.*

Sitting in my sanctuary—in a brown wooden chair, at a brown wooden desk—a radical transformation occurred. "God, I choose to believe! If this worked for Nebuchadnezzar, this will work for me." *Choosing to look up,* my faith focus shifted from my temporal circumstances to my eternal resources.

In that moment . . . I changed.

The change proved genuine. My circumstances remained challenging. The needs of my family only escalated. And life's speed still raced at full throttle. Yet, I experienced ongoing victory from being controlled by my circumstances and pushed around by my problems.

Yes, on a cold Communist morning, God highlighted one verse with His holy illumination: *"I raised my eyes toward heaven, and my sanity was restored."* In my concrete cubicle, I learned a lesson for life: To look down is to be discouraged.

To look around is to be disappointed.

To look within is to be disillusioned.

To look up is to see Him!

You and I are prone to look down and be discouraged, to look around and be disappointed, to look within and be disillusioned. Yet, in looking up, we see Him, our Deliverer, and we are delivered.

Since that time, other Scriptures have become dear in urging me to turn my eyes up and upon Him. Where will I look? Where will I fix my gaze? Where is my focus of faith? I must make the supernatural choice.

Psalm 121:1-2:

"I lift up my eyes to the mountains —

where does my help come from?

"My help comes from the Lord,

the Maker of heaven and earth."

Hebrews 12:2a:

"Fixing our eyes on Jesus, the pioneer and perfecter of faith."

A ballerina, when performing pirouettes, fixes her focus on a single spot on the wall. This technique, known as spotting, provides a constant orientation of her head and eyes to enhance her control and prevent dizziness.

A sea captain at the helm of a vessel fixes his focus on the beams of a lighthouse to aid navigation. Situational awareness equips him to avoid shallow waters and treacherous rocks.

God gives specific instructions regarding our fixed focus of faith. This focus is a Person, Jesus. We are clearly told to fix our eyes on Him, the Author and the Perfecter of our faith.

I want to shout upon applying the teaching from Harvest Bible Chapel's pastor James MacDonald on 2 Chronicles 20:12. When armies of adversity threaten to take me down, I declare with determination: *Lord, I can't fix it or fight it or figure it out, but my eyes are on You* (2 Chronicles 20:12).

Supernatural promises and a supernatural choice, at long last, bring us to consider:

Supernatural Outcome

His supernatural promises plus our supernatural choices formulate a supernatural equation. The result delivers a supernatural outcome, a holy combustion of resources that the world cannot copy or contain.

To be who you want to be, to do what you are called to do, requires a belief system beyond yourself. Your greatest priority in life must be a Person, not a program or a plan. Your highest calling is to develop an intimate relationship with Jesus. He is the living Word and He points us to the written Word. A life in superlatives awaits the woman who decides: I will depend on His presence, His protection, and His provision. I will, by faith, fix my focus on Him.

Yes, He is the Alpha and the Omega of life and of this book. From cover to cover He has been the theme. In the beginning, we discussed identity, intimacy, and growth. Here at the end, we discussed His supernatural promises. Everything in between made Him our focus—Jesus for the leader's wife.

As you pursue your goal, living with eternal intentionality, I implore you to live desperately dependent on Him. Then you will declare with the psalmist: "We went through fire and water, but you brought us to a place of abundance" (Psalm 66:12). That place of abundance is a Person, our Alpha and Omega.

'Tis so sweet to trust in Jesus,
And to take Him at His Word;
Just to rest upon His promise,
And to know, "Thus says the Lord!"
Jesus, Jesus, how I trust Him!
How I've proved Him o'er and o'er
Jesus, Jesus, precious Jesus!
O for grace to trust Him more!
O how sweet to trust in Jesus,
Just to trust His cleansing blood;
And in simple faith to plunge me
'Neath the healing, cleansing flood!
Jesus, Jesus, how I trust Him!
How I've proved Him o'er and o'er
Jesus, Jesus, precious Jesus!
O for grace to trust Him more!
Yes, 'tis sweet to trust in Jesus,
Just from sin and self to cease;
Just from Jesus simply taking
Life and rest, and joy and peace.
Jesus, Jesus, how I trust Him!
How I've proved Him o'er and o'er
Jesus, Jesus, precious Jesus!
O for grace to trust Him more!
I'm so glad I learned to trust Thee,
Precious Jesus, Savior, Friend;
And I know that Thou art with me,
Wilt be with me to the end.

– Louis Steed, 1882

Living with Eternal Intentionality™

"Not to us, Lord, not to us but to your name be the glory, because of your love and faithfulness" (Psalm 115:1).

Looking back, which chapter was your favorite? Why?

Which lesson has been your greatest? How will you make its application to your life?

What one heart-felt principle will you share with another leader's wife?

What does it mean to you, as the leader's wife, to live with eternal intentionality?

From reading this book, how have you grown:

In intimacy with Jesus?

In authenticity with others?

In a passion for your calling?

In a purpose for your influence?

Cameo

This one's for you, my dear reader. Your life is a story, which deserves to be told. As your love for Jesus grows, and as your pursuit of intimacy with Him increases, you will write for His glory, a story of which the world is not worthy.

I love you, and praise God for the privilege of sharing life through these pages.

As we prepare to close the back cover, I urge you to make Mark 12:30 your personal mission statement:

"Love the Lord your God with all your heart and with all your soul and with all your mind and with all your strength."

Out of that mission statement,

I pray you love your husband with a fiery, passionate, supernatural, godly, Holy Spirit-inspired, partnership love, and that you walk right beside him, hand in hand, heart to heart, marching into a world that desperately needs Jesus.

My prayer for you as you eagerly embrace the life that God has given you is the blessing found in Numbers 6:24-26:

"The Lord bless you, and keep you; The Lord make His face shine on you, and be gracious to you; The Lord lift up His countenance on you, and give you peace" (NASB).

Amen.

APPENDIX

Who I Am in Christ

I Am Accepted

John 1:12	I am God's child.
John 15:15	I am Christ's friend.
Romans 5:1	I have been justified.
1 Corinthians 6:17	I am united with the Lord, and I am one spirit with Him.
1 Corinthians 6:20	I have been bought with a price. I belong to God.
1 Corinthians 12:27	I am a member of Christ's Body.
Ephesians 1:1	I am a saint.
Ephesians 1:5	I have been adopted as God's child.
Ephesians 2:18	I have direct access to God through the Holy Spirit.
Colossians 1:14	I have been redeemed and forgiven of all my sins.
Colossians 2:10	I am complete in Christ.

I Am Secure

Romans 8:1-2	I am free from condemnation.
Romans 8:28	I am assured all things work together for good.
Romans 8:31-34	I am free from any condemning charges against me.
Romans 8:35-39	I cannot be separated from the love of God.
2 Corinthians 1:21-22	I have been established, anointed and sealed by God.
Philippians 1:6	I am confident that the good work God has begun in me will be perfected.
Philippians 3:20	I am a citizen of heaven.
Colossians 3:3	I am hidden with Christ in God.
2 Timothy 1:7	I have not been given a spirit of fear, but of power, love and a sound mind.
Hebrews 4:16	I can find grace and mercy in time of need.
1 John 5:18	I am born of God and the evil one cannot touch me.

I Am Significant

Matthew 5:13-14	I am the salt and light of the earth.
John 15:1,5	I am a branch of the true vine, a channel of His life.
John 15:16	I have been chosen and appointed to bear fruit.
Acts 1:8	I am a personal witness of Christ.
1 Corinthians 3:16	I am God's temple.
2 Corinthians 5:17-21	I am a minister of reconciliation for God.
2 Corinthians 6:1	I am God's coworker (see 1 Corinthians 3:9).
Ephesians 2:6	I am seated with Christ in the heavenly realm.
Ephesians 2:10	I am God's workmanship.
Ephesians 3:12	I may approach God with freedom and confidence.
Philippians 4:13	I can do all things through Christ who strengthens me.

Victory Over the Darkness written by Neil T. Anderson, © 2017 Bethany House, a division of Baker Publishing Group. Used by permission.

Would You Like to
Know God Personally?

The message found in this booklet has been warmly received by millions of people around the world! Individuals of all ages, religious backgrounds, and ethnicities have found the message contained in this booklet to be personally helpful in their relationship with God. We hope that you are blessed by it and will pass it along to others!

1. God loves you and created you to know Him personally. He has a wonderful plan for your life.

God's Love

"For God so loved the world that He gave His one and only Son, that whoever believes in Him shall not perish but have eternal life." (John 3:16)

God's Plan

"Now this is eternal life: that they may know You, the only true God, and Jesus Christ, whom You have sent." (John 17:3)

What prevents us from knowing God personally?

2. *People are sinful and separated from God, so we cannot know Him personally or experience His love.*

People Are Sinful

"...all have sinned and fall short of the glory of God" (Romans 3:23)

People were created to have fellowship with God; but, because of our stubborn self-will, we chose to go our own independent way and fellowship with God was broken. This self-will, characterized by an attitude of active rebellion or passive indifference, is evidence of what the Bible calls sin.

People Are Separated

"For the wages of sin is death..." [spiritual separation from God] (Romans 6:23)

GOD

Our Condition

This diagram illustrates that God is holy and people are sinful. A great chasm separates the two. The arrows illustrate that we are continually trying to reach God and establish a personal relationship with Him through our own efforts, such as a good life, philosophy or religion, but we inevitably fail.

The third principle explains the only way to bridge this gap...

PEOPLE

3. Jesus Christ is God's only provision for man's sin. Through Him alone we can know God personally and experience His love and plan.

He Died in Our Place

"But God demonstrates His own love for us in this: While we were still sinners, Christ died for us." (Romans 5:8)

He Rose From the Dead

"...Christ died for our sins...He was buried...He was raised on the third day according to the Scriptures...He appeared to Peter, then to the Twelve. After that He appeared to more than five hundred..." (1 Corinthians 15:3-6)

He Is the Only Way to God

"Jesus said to him, 'I am the way, and the truth, and the life; no one comes to the Father, but through Me.'" (John 14:6)

GOD

JESUS

PEOPLE

God's Response

This diagram illustrates that God has bridged the chasm that separates us from Him by sending His Son, Jesus Christ, to die on the cross in our place to pay the penalty for our sins.

The fourth principle explains it's not enough to just know these truths...

4. We must individually receive Jesus Christ as Savior and Lord; then we can know God personally and experience His love and plan for us.

We Must Receive Christ

"Yet to all who received Him, to those who believed in His name, He gave the right to become children of God." (John 1:12)

We Receive Christ Through Faith

"For it is by grace you have been saved, through faith — and this not from yourselves, it is the gift of God — not by works, so that no one can boast." (Ephesians 2:8-9)

When We Receive Christ, We Experience a New Birth

(Read John 3:1-8)

Our Response

We Receive Christ by Personal Invitation

[Christ speaking] "'Here I am! I stand at the door and knock. If anyone hears My voice and opens the door, I will come in and eat with him, and he with Me.'" (Revelation 3:20)

Receiving Christ involves turning to God from self (repentance) and trusting Christ to come into our lives to forgive us of our sins and to make us what He wants us to be. Just to agree intellectually that Jesus Christ is the Son of God and that He died on the cross for our sins is not enough. Nor is it enough to have an emotional experience. We receive Jesus Christ by faith, as an act of our will.

These two circles represent two kinds of lives.

A life entrusted to Christ. Christ is central and on the throne, and self yields to Christ.

A life without Jesus Christ. Self is central and on the throne and Jesus Christ (†) is on the outside.

Prayer Is Talking with God

You Can Receive Christ Right Now by Prayer through Faith

God knows your heart and is not as concerned with your words as He is with the attitude of your heart. The following is a suggested prayer:

Lord Jesus, I want to know You personally. Thank You for dying on the cross for my sins. I open the door of my life and receive You as my Savior and Lord. Thank You for forgiving me of my sins and giving me eternal life. Make me the kind of person You want me to be.

Does This Prayer Express the Desire of Your Heart?

If it does, pray this prayer right now, and Christ will come into your life, as He promised.

How to Know That Christ Is in Your Life

Did You Receive Christ into Your Life?

According to His promise as recorded in Revelation 3:20, where is Christ right now in relation to you? Christ said that He would come into your life and be your Savior and friend so you can know Him personally. Would He mislead you? On what authority do you know that God has answered your prayer? (The trustworthiness of God Himself and His Word.)

The Bible Promises Eternal Life to All Who Receive Christ

"And this is the testimony: God has given us eternal life, and this life is in His Son. Whoever has the Son has life; whoever does not have the Son of God does not have life. I write these things to you who believe in the name of the Son of God so that you may know that you have eternal life." (1 John 5:11-13)

Thank God often that Christ is in your life and that He will never leave you (Hebrews 13:5). You can know on the basis of His promise that Christ lives in you and that you have eternal life from the very moment you invite Him in.

Do Not Depend on Feelings

The promise of God's Word, the Bible — not our feelings — is our authority. The Christian lives by faith (trust) in the character of God Himself and His Word. This train diagram illustrates the relationship among fact (God and His Word), faith (our trust in God and His Word), and feeling (the result of our faith and obedience) (John 14:21).

The train will run with or without the caboose. However, it would be useless to attempt to pull the train by the caboose. In the same way, we as Christians do not depend on feelings or emotions, but we place our faith (trust) in the character of God and the promises of His Word.

Fact — Faith — Feeling

Now That You Have Entered Into a Personal Relationship With Christ

The moment you received Christ by faith, as an act of your will, many things happened, including the following:

- Christ came into your life (Revelation 3:20 and Colossians 1:27)
- Your sins were forgiven (Colossians 1:14)
- You became a child of God (John 1:12)
- You received eternal life (John 5:24)
- You began the great adventure for which God created you (John 10:10; 2 Corinthians 5:17 and 1 Thessalonians 5:18)

Can you think of anything more wonderful that could happen to you than entering into a personal relationship with Jesus Christ? Would you like to thank God in prayer right now for what He has done for you? By thanking God, you demonstrate your faith.

To enjoy your new relationship with God...

Suggestions for Christian Growth

Spiritual growth results from trusting Jesus Christ. "...The righteous will live by faith" (Galatians 3:11). A life of faith will enable you to trust God increasingly with every detail of your life, and to practice the following:

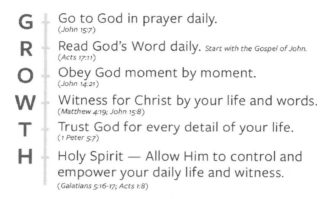

G Go to God in prayer daily.
(John 15:7)

R Read God's Word daily. Start with the Gospel of John.
(Acts 17:11)

O Obey God moment by moment.
(John 14:21)

W Witness for Christ by your life and words.
(Matthew 4:19; John 15:8)

T Trust God for every detail of your life.
(1 Peter 5:7)

H Holy Spirit — Allow Him to control and empower your daily life and witness.
(Galatians 5:16-17; Acts 1:8)

Fellowship in a Good Church

Several logs burn brightly together, but put one aside on the cold hearth and the fire goes out. So it is with your relationship with other Christians. If you do not belong to a church, do not wait to be invited. Take the initiative; call the pastor of a nearby church where Christ is honored and His Word is preached. Start this week, and make plans to attend regularly.

Remember...

Your walk with Christ depends on what you allow Him to do in and through you, empowered by the Holy Spirit, not what you do for Him through self-effort.

For more information about a relationship with God and growing in your spiritual life, consider visiting:

www.Cru.org

www.EveryPerson.com

www.EveryStudent.com

www.StartingWithGod.com

If you found the message in this booklet helpful, please let us know! We'd love to hear your story!

Please email us at Cru@Cru.org

Satisfied?

Satisfaction: (n.) fulfillment of one's needs, longings, or desires

What words would you use to describe your current experience as a Christian?

Growing	Frustrated
Disappointing	Fulfilled
Forgiven	Stuck
Struggling	Joyful
Defeated	Exciting
Up and down	Empty
Discouraged	Duty
Intimate	Mediocre
Painful	Dynamic
Guilty	Vital
So-so	Others?

Do you desire more? Jesus said, "If anyone is thirsty, let him come to me and drink. Whoever believes in me, as the Scripture has said, streams of living water will flow from within him" (John 7:37, 38).

What did Jesus mean? John, the biblical author, went on to explain, "By this he meant the Spirit, whom those who believed in him were later to receive. Up to that time the Spirit had not been given, since Jesus had not yet been glorified" (John 7:39).

Jesus promised that God's Holy Spirit would satisfy the thirst, or deepest longings, of all who believe in Jesus Christ. However, many Christians do not understand the Holy Spirit or how to experience Him in their daily lives.

The Divine Gift

Divine: (adj.) given by God

God has given us His Spirit so that we can experience intimacy with Him and enjoy all He has for us.

The Holy Spirit is the source of our deepest satisfaction.

The Holy Spirit is God's permanent presence with us.
Jesus said, "I will ask the Father, and he will give you another Counselor to be with you forever—the Spirit of truth" (John 14:16, 17).

The Holy Spirit enables us to understand and experience all God has given us.
"We have not received the spirit of the world but the Spirit who is from God, that we may understand what God has freely given us" (1 Corinthians 2:12).

The Holy Spirit enables us to experience many things:

- o   A genuine new spiritual life (John 3:1–8).
- o   The assurance of being a child of God (Romans 8:15, 16).
- o   The infinite love of God (Romans 5:5; Ephesians 3:18, 19).

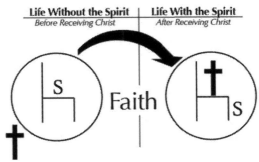

Life Without the Spirit	Life With the Spirit
Before Receiving Christ	*After Receiving Christ*

"The man without the Spirit does not accept the things that come from the Spirit of God, for they are foolishness to him, and he cannot understand them, because they are spiritually discerned" (1 Corinthians 2:14).

"The spiritual man makes judgments about all things…We have the mind of Christ" (1 Corinthians 2:15, 16).
"But those who are controlled by the Holy Spirit think about things that please the Spirit" (Romans 8:5, NLT).

The Present Danger

Danger: (n.) a thing that may cause injury, loss, or pain

We cannot experience intimacy with God and enjoy all He has for us if we fail to depend on His Spirit.

People who trust in their own efforts and strength to live the Christian life will experience failure and frustration, as will those who live to please themselves rather than God.

We cannot live the Christian life in our own strength.

"Are you so foolish? After beginning with the Spirit, are you now trying to attain your goal by human effort?" (Galatians 3:3).

We cannot enjoy all God desires for us if we live by our self-centered desires.

"For the sinful nature desires what is contrary to the Spirit, and the Spirit what is contrary to the sinful nature. They are in conflict with each other, so that you do not do what you want" (Galatians 5:17).

Three Kinds of Lifestyles

A Self-centered Life	A Christ-centered Life	A Self-centered Life
Before Receiving Christ	*After Receiving Christ*	

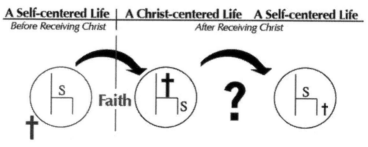

"Brothers, I could not address you as spiritual, but as worldly—mere infants in Christ. I gave you milk, not solid food, for you were not yet ready for it. Indeed, you are still not ready. You are still worldly. For since there is jealousy and quarreling among you, are you not worldly? Are you not acting like mere men?" (1 Corinthians 3:1–3).

The Intimate Journey

Journey: (n.) any course from one experience to another

By walking in the Spirit we increasingly experience intimacy with God and enjoy all He has for us.

Walking in the Spirit moment by moment is a lifestyle. It is learning to depend upon the Holy Spirit for His abundant resources as a way of life.

As we walk in the Spirit, we have the ability to live a life pleasing to God.

"So I say, live by the Spirit, and you will not gratify the desires of the sinful nature... Since we live by the Spirit, let us keep in step with the Spirit" (Galatians 5:16, 25).

As we walk in the Spirit, we experience intimacy with God and all He has for us.

"But the fruit of the Spirit is love, joy, peace, patience, kindness, goodness, faithfulness, gentleness and self-control" (Galatians 5:22, 23).

The Christ-centered Life

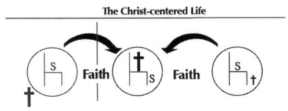

Faith (trust in God and His promises) is the only way a Christian can live by the Spirit.

Spiritual breathing is a powerful word picture which can help you experience moment-by-moment dependence upon the Spirit.

Exhale: Confess your sin the moment you become aware of it—agree with God concerning it and thank Him for His forgiveness, according to 1 John 1:9 and Hebrews 10:1–25. Confession requires repentance—a change in attitude and action.

Inhale: Surrender control of your life to Christ, and rely upon the Holy Spirit to fill you with His presence and power by faith, according to His command (Ephesians 5:18) and promise (1 John 5:14, 15).

» How does the Holy Spirit fill us with His power?

The Empowering Presence

Empower: (v.) to give ability to

We are filled with the Spirit by faith, enabling us to experience intimacy with God and enjoy all He has for us.

The essence of the Christian life is what God does in and through us, not what we do for God. Christ's life is reproduced in the believer by the power of the Holy Spirit. To be filled with the Spirit is to be directed and empowered by Him.

By faith, we experience God's power through the Holy Spirit.

"I pray that out of his glorious riches he may strengthen you with power through his Spirit in your inner being, so that Christ may dwell in your hearts through faith" (Ephesians 3:16, 17).

Three important questions to ask yourself:

1. Am I ready now to surrender control of my life to our Lord Jesus Christ? (Romans 12:1, 2).
2. Am I ready now to confess my sins? (1 John 1:9). Sin grieves God's Spirit (Ephesians 4:30). But God in His love has forgiven all of your sins—past, present, and future—because Christ has died for you.
3. Do I sincerely desire to be directed and empowered by the Holy Spirit? (John 7:37–39).

By faith claim the fullness of the Spirit according to His command and promise:

God **COMMANDS** us to be filled with the Spirit.

"...be filled with the Spirit" (Ephesians 5:18).

God **PROMISES** He will always answer when we pray according to His will.

"This is the confidence we have in approaching God: that if we ask anything according to his will, he hears us. And if we know that he hears us—whatever we ask—we know that we have what we asked of him" (1 John 5:14, 15).

» How to pray to be filled with the Holy Spirit...

The Turning Point

Turning point: time when a decisive change occurs

We are filled with the Holy Spirit by faith alone.

Sincere prayer is one way of expressing our faith. The following is a suggested prayer:

Dear Father, I need You. I acknowledge that I have sinned against You by directing my own life. I thank You that You have forgiven my sins through Christ's death on the cross for me. I now invite Christ to again take His place on the throne of my life. Fill me with the Holy Spirit as You commanded me to be filled, and as You promised in Your Word that You would do if I asked in faith. I pray this in the name of Jesus. I now thank You for filling me with the Holy Spirit and directing my life.

Does this prayer express the desire of your heart? If so, you can pray right now and trust God to fill you with His Holy Spirit.

How to know that you are filled by the Holy Spirit

o   Did you ask God to fill you with the Holy Spirit?
o   Do you know that you are now filled with the Holy Spirit?
o   On what authority? (On the trustworthiness of God Himself and His Word: Hebrews 11:6; Romans 14:22, 23.)

As you continue to depend on God's Spirit moment by moment you will experience and enjoy intimacy with God and all He has for you—a truly rich and satisfying life.

An important reminder…

Do Not Depend on Feelings

The promise of God's Word, the Bible—not our feelings—is our authority. The Christian lives by faith (trust) in the trustworthiness of God Himself and His Word. Flying in an airplane can illustrate the relationship among fact (God and His Word), faith (our trust in God and His Word), and feeling (the result of our faith and obedience) (John 14:21).

To be transported by an airplane, we must place our faith in the trustworthiness of the aircraft and the pilot who flies it. Our feelings of confidence or fear do not affect the ability of the airplane to transport us, though they do affect how much we enjoy the trip. In the same way, we as Christians do not depend on feelings or emotions, but we place our faith (trust) in the trustworthiness of God and the promises of His Word.

Now That You are Filled with the Holy Spirit

Thank God that the Spirit will enable you:

- o   To glorify Christ with your life (John 16:14).
- o   To grow in your understanding of God and His Word (1 Corinthians 2:14, 15).
- o   To live a life pleasing to God (Galatians 5:16–23).

Remember the promise of Jesus:

"But you will receive power when the Holy Spirit comes on you; and you will be my witnesses in Jerusalem, and in all Judea and Samaria, and to the ends of the earth" (Acts 1:8).

If you would like additional resources on the Holy Spirit, please go to www.crustore.org

NOTES

1. Neil Anderson with Joanne Anderson. *Daily in Christ, A Devotional.* Eugene, OR: Harvest House Publishers, 1993. Print.

2. Brennon Manning. *Abba's Child.* Colorado Springs, CO: NavPress, 2002. Print.

3. Edith Deen. *Great Women of the Christian Faith.* Westwood, NJ: Barbour and Company, Inc., 1959. Print. (Paraphrase and quotations)

4. Warren W. Wiersbe. *50 People Every Christian Should Know.* Grand Rapids, MI: Baker, 2009. Print.

5. Arthur Bennett. *Valley of Vision.* Carlisle, PA: The Banner of Truth Trust, 1975. Print.

6. Elisabeth Elliot. *Gateway to Joy: Reflections That Draw Us Nearer To God.* Ann Arbor, MI: Servant Publications, 1998. Print.

7. Warren W. Wiersbe. *The Bible Expository Commentary.* Vol. 2, Wheaton, IL: Victor Books, 1989. Print

8. *"Celebrating the Life of Ruth Bell Graham-Billy Graham's Wife."* YouTube. Oct. 11, 2011. June 12, 2012. https://www.youtube.com/watch?v=9ln3qXoroAs (Paraphrase and quotations)

9. Patricia Cornwell. *Ruth, a Portrait: The Story of Ruth Bell Graham.* New York, NY: Doubleday, 1997. Print.

10. S. Thomas. (2012, February 4). It's me. [Web log comment]. Retrieved from http://benandsusiethomas.com

11. Evelyn Wittner. *Abigail Adams: First Lady of Faith and Courage.* Fenton, MI: Mott Media, LLC, 1976. Print.

12. David McCullough. *John Adams.* New York, NY: Simon & Schuster, 2001. Print. (Content quoted and paraphrased).

13. Roger Steer. *George Müller: Delighted In God.* Ross-shire, Great Britain: Christian Focus Publications, Ltd., 2008. Print. (Content quoted and paraphrased).

14. C.S. Lewis. *Mere Christianity.* New York, NY: HarperCollins, 1952. Print.

15. Bob Beltz and Walt Kallestad. *World-Changers: Live to Serve.* Wheaton, IL: Tyndale, 2007. Print.

16. "*Celebrating the Life of Ruth Bell Graham-Billy Graham's Wife.*" YouTube. Oct. 11, 2011. June 12, 2012. https://www.youtube.com/watch?v=9ln3qXor0As

17. Bobb Biehl. *Master-Planning: A Complete Guide for Building a Strategic Plan for Your Business, Church, or Organization.* Nashville, TN: B & H Publishing Group, 1997. Print.

18. *Walk the Line.* Directed by James Mangold, Performances by Joaquin Phoenix, Reese Witherspoon, Ginnifer Goodwin, 20th Century Fox, 2005.

19. Dallas Willard. *The Divine Conspiracy: Rediscovering Our Hidden Life in God.* New York, NY: HarperCollins, 1998. Print.

20. Pepper Schwartz. "The Way of the Affair: the Science and Psychology of Infidelity." *On Point.* NPR. WUFC-FM, *Orlando.* 14 Nov. 2012.

21. Laura Bush. *Spoken From the Heart.* New York, NY: Simon & Schuster (Scribner), 2010. Print.

ABOUT THE AUTHOR

Debby Thompson and her husband, Larry, have served in global missions with Campus Crusade for Christ International (Cru®) since 1974, and are counted among the pioneering Western missionaries who lived covertly behind the Iron Curtain in Communist-controlled Poland. In total, the Thompsons spent 33 years in Eastern Europe, ultimately leading Cru's work in 20 European nations. Together with their three children, they were witnesses to a period of dramatic social, political, and spiritual change.

Now living in Cincinnati, Ohio, Debby serves on the Global Leadership Council of Athletes in Action®, Cru's sports ministry. An active grandmother of six, she is also a sought-after speaker, writer, and mentor for women around the world. Debby's new book, entitled *The Leader's Wife: Living with Eternal Intentionality*, encourages women to pursue intimacy with Jesus, authenticity with others, a passion for their calling, and a purpose for their influence.

Subscribe to Debby's blog, *Living with Eternal Intentionality*™, *GPS for a Woman of Purpose*™ at DebbyThompson.com, and follow her on Twitter at *@Debbythompson17*. To contact her directly, email: Debby. thompson@cru.org.

ACKNOWLEDGMENTS

My heartfelt appreciation goes to a choice group of individuals whom God orchestrated to bring this book to life.

Linda Dillow: Thank you, my delightful mentor, for your vision and enthusiasm toward this book. You are the epitome of encouragement. Our Cold War friendship still warms my heart.

Bunny Fisher: Thank you for your unselfish investment of time and professional guidance with the manuscript when the book was only a distant dream.

Jane Glenchur: Thank you for reviewing the manuscript and making insightful improvements; your keen eye for detail is a rare gift.

Emily Graf: Thank you for your kindness and competence, which coalesce beautifully with your administrative gifts.

Matt Kavgian: Thank you for your advice and wise counsel; my questions were always safe with you.

Joan Parsons: Thank you for infusing the process with your encouraging feedback.

Rich Wiewiora: Thank you for raising the bar of excellence with your expertise; your work was pivotal.

Cheryl Winget: Thank you for confirming my use of music terminology in Chapter 9.

Les Stobbe: Thank you, as my agent, for your steadfast advocacy, support and guidance.

COO Anna Raats, Creative Director Hannah Nichols, and the Ambassador International publishing team: Thank you for giving my book a home. It was a joy to work with all of you.

My Precious Family: Thank you Larry, Anne Coleman, Matt, David, Blake, Grace, Matt, Sophia, Grace, Sabrina, Vera, David, Faye, and Dorothy Faye (Mama); you are God's sweetest of earthly gifts to me, and I love you dearly. For this book, we waited and prayed together.

For more information about
Debby Thompson
&
The Leader's Wife

please visit:

DebbyThompson.com
@Debbythompson17
Instagram: Debbythompson17

For more information about
AMBASSADOR INTERNATIONAL
please visit:

www.ambassador-international.com
@AmbassadorIntl
www.facebook.com/AmbassadorIntl

If you enjoyed this book, please consider leaving us a review on
Amazon, Goodreads, or our website.

Made in the USA
Columbia, SC
25 February 2024

32256101R00098